"Out of all of my sisters and brothers, I have always known that there was something special about Shirley."
—Lina Caesar Brown

"My sister Shirley not only afforded me the wonderful privilege of traveling and singing with her, but it was through her ministry that I totally surrendered my life to the Lord. I am very proud that she is my sister and my pastor."
—Anne Caesar Price

"My baby sister Shirley is blessed not only because she loves the Lord with all her heart, but because she sincerely loves all mankind."
—Julius E. Caesar

"By the time Shirley was born, I had already moved away from home, but I would often bring her over to spend the night with me. No one could have told me that my little sister would one day sing for presidents, governors, and heads of state. I am very proud of her."
—Virginia Caesar Reed

"I thank God for my sister Shirley's success. Her singing ministry has been a blessing to our entire family."
—Cleo Caesar

"At the age of ten years old, my quartet was the first singing group that Shirley traveled with. After she performed, it was very difficult for us to follow her. God bless you, Baby Sis, you are the greatest."

—LeRoy Caesar

"Shirley has richly touched my life in countless ways. Needless to say that I have gained added respect simply by saying she is my sister. I love you."

—Solomon Caesar

"I had the privilege of sharing in the early years of Shirley's life when, at the age of twelve, she sang with Leroy Johnson. Her mom, my sister, always sent me along to be her chaperone."

—Aunt Ida Davis

SHIRLEY

THE LADY, THE MELODY, & THE WORD

THE INSPIRATIONAL STORY OF THE FIRST LADY OF GOSPEL

CAESAR

THOMAS NELSON PUBLISHERS
Nashville
Printed in the United States of America

Published in Nashville, Tennessee, by Thomas Nelson, Inc., Publishers.

Unless otherwise noted, the Bible version used in this publication is THE NEW KING JAMES VERSION. Copyright © 1979, 1980, 1982, 1990, Thomas Nelson, Inc., Publishers.

Scripture quotations noted KJV are from THE KING JAMES VERSION of the Bible.

Library of Congress Cataloging-in-Publication Data
Caesar, Shirley, 1938–
    The lady, the melody, and the word : the Shirley Caesar story /
Shirley Caesar.
        p.   cm.
    ISBN 0-7852-7155-4
    1. Caesar, Shirley, 1938–   . 2. Gospel musicians—United States—
Biography.   3. Christian biography—United States.   I. Title.
ML420.C175A3   1998
782.25'4'092—dc21   97–51908
                                                                            CIP
                                                                            MN

Printed in the United States of America.

1 2 3 4 5 6 BVG 03 02 01 00 99 98

CONTENTS

This book is dedicated to the memory of my beloved mother, Hallie Martin Caesar, whose love gave me my life purpose and direction; my father, Jim Caesar, who left me such a profound musical legacy; my sisters Lucille, Gertrude, and Joyce and my brother Albert who have all gone to be with the Lord. I thank God for allowing their lives to impact mine in such a positive way. I look forward to our reunion in heaven.

I dedicate this book as well to my sister Virginia and my brother Julius, both of whom persistently encouraged me to excel and to be all that I could be; to my brother LeRoy who allowed me to travel and sing with his quartet when I was only ten years old; my sister Lina and my brother Cleo who protected and sheltered me as I was growing up; my brother Solomon who at ten years old was playfully preaching a mock sermon in our backyard and encouraged me to shout the name of Jesus three times (what began as child's play became very serious, and as a result, that day I received Christ into my life); and my sister Anne who forfeited her own dreams and aspirations to labor in my ministry. She has always been there for me.

ACKNOWLEDGMENTS

THE Scripture says in Jeremiah 1:5: "Before I formed thee in the belly I knew thee; and before thou camest forth out of the womb I sanctified thee, and I ordained thee a prophet unto the nations" (KJV).

There is no greater honor that you can have bestowed upon you than to be chosen and annointed by God as a vessel to minister His Word to His people. My life is one of divine destiny and purpose. Every road that I have traveled, every success and failure that I have experienced, and every person who has entered my life has been ordained by God. Nothing happens by chance, it is all according to God's timing. It never ceases to amaze me how the Lord will place people in your life just when you need them the most.

There are few key people I would like to acknowledge, whom the Lord has placed in my life to not only help from the framework for this book, but also to assist me in fulfilling the purpose to which I have been called.

To my wonderful husband, Bishop Harold Ivory Williams, whom I love very much. Thank you for being my constant source of strength, inspiration, and encouragement.

To the Caesar Singers, past and present, thank you for sticking by me through the good times and the bad times, traveling with me across the length and breadth of this country proclaiming the gospel of good news to countless thousands of souls. Great shall be your reward in heaven.

To my church family, Mount Calvary Word of Faith Church, thank you for allowing me to be your pastor. I promise I will never make you ashamed. I love you!

To Word Records, Gospel Division—namely Roland Lundy, Chuck Myricks, Skip Barrett, Marvie Wright, and Bill Lee—I appreciate each of you standing by me and supporting my ministry.

To Dr. Deborah Graham and Dr. Brooksie Harrington, thank you for your invaluable input.

To Angel Wiley, a very special god-daughter, thank you for the many hours you spent assisting in the editing of the final manuscript. I love you!

To Corey Bizzell, thank you for picking up the slack and working long and diligently in the office while Carolyn and I burned the midnight oil writing this book. I appreciate your hard work.

To Michael Mathis, a dedicated and faithful friend. You are such an annointed prolific musician and songwriter. You always come through when I need you the most. Thank you for the use of your lyrics on some of the introductions to the chapters of this book.

To my manager and friend, Carolyn Sanders, as Joshua was to Moses, so you are to me. Thank you for being my right hand. We make an awesome team. I am convinced that whatever we set our minds to do, by the annointing of the Holy Spirit, we can do it.

CHAPTER ONE

Running for Jesus

THE MELODY

Don't look to the left, neither look to the right
look straight ahead, keep yours eyes on Christ,
all that glitters, it just ain't gold,
don't let nobody cause you to lose your soul.

The Lord will help you to keep on moving on.
Move on up a little higher, get all excited get on fire
there's no time for you to stop,
keep on reaching until you reach the top.

The Lord will help you to keep moving on.
—"Keep on Moving"

∷∷∷∷∷∷∷∷∷ AND THE WORD ∷∷∷∷∷∷∷∷∷

In You, O LORD, I put my trust;
Let me never be ashamed;
Deliver me in Your righteousness.
Bow down Your ear to me,
Deliver me speedily;
Be my rock of refuge,
A fortress of defense to save me.
—Psalm 31:1–2

————— HAVE you ever been in a predicament where you knew your very life was in jeopardy? I mean, a situation or an incident that caused you to see your whole life flash in front of your eyes and made you keenly aware that without divine intervention your days, hours, minutes, even seconds remaining on this earth were limited? A situation quite similar to when a car suddenly pulls out in front of you and there is no way humanly possible to avoid the impending collision? Or when you are a passenger in an airplane that suddenly encounters severe turbulence and begins dipping and diving and without warning drops a hundred feet?

I have had many such experiences in my life where I knew the hand of God was protecting me, but one incident stands out in my mind above all others. I remember it so vividly because I was just a teenager when it occurred. The year was 1954; the United States Supreme Court had just voted to end segregation in the South. I grew up during an era when racism, sexism, and prejudice were very prevalent. When the Supreme Court ruled that this practice was unconstitutional, many people were angry about that decision.

At the time I was already a gospel singer and had been since the age of eight. I had begun traveling locally on weekends to churches in Raleigh, Greensboro, Chapel Hill, Winston-Salem, and other surrounding North and South Carolina cities with either my pastor, Bishop Frizelle Yelverton, my neighbors, Mother Mary Jones and Mother Stella Williams, or Thelma Bumpass and the Royalettes. Quite often my mother would send my Aunt Ida or my brother Cleo to accompany me on these weekend appearances. I was small in stature, very petite, and wore my hair in braids. When I sang they had to stand me either on a box or a table. As a result, people nicknamed me "Baby Shirley." On one such occasion after singing at a church in Winston-Salem, North Carolina, a gospel announcer, Leroy Johnson, who was also a gospel singer, was so touched that he invited me to return the following Sunday to sing on his radio program. The response was so phenomenal that Leroy kept inviting me again and again. Eventually we began singing in churches together all across the southern states. We were known as "Leroy Johnson and Baby Shirley Caesar."

Early one Saturday, around 3:00 A.M., we were driving down Highway 15, coming from a concert in Tarboro, North Carolina, en route to another one scheduled the next night in Columbia, South Carolina. I was traveling with Leroy Johnson, Reverend and Mrs. Jackson, and another missionary and her seventeen-year-old nephew. The sky was darker than usual. Reverend Jackson was driving the car. He and I had been discussing numerous biblical issues for hours but were unable to agree on very many of them. He felt that since he was older, I should just concede to everything he said. But even as a teenager, I would not, could not, compromise my beliefs. Our discussion kept everyone awake most of the night. Gradually the intensity of our conversation began to decline, and we concluded that we would simply agree to disagree. As we continued down Highway 15, the calmness of the night, along with the humming of the car engine, slowly made everyone drowsy. Reverend Jackson started yawning. I talked to him for a few more minutes, but then I started yawning also. Reverend Jackson tried to continue driving, but it was obvious that he was getting very sleepy. In the distance, he saw a service station, and he thought this would be the opportune time to fill the car with gas and allow everyone to refresh themselves. As we drove into the station, I was immediately gripped with a feeling of uneasiness. The place was eerie in appearance; it was a dingy, old white building with a rusty sign hanging from the side of it. The driveway was unpaved and filled with muddy potholes. There was only one gas pump in front of this dilapidated building. The place looked sinister, but we had to stop because, even though it was only two miles to the next town, Bennettsville, South Carolina, Reverend Jackson was too exhausted to proceed without refreshing himself. Reverend Jackson turned to the rest of our group and said, "Everybody wake up, better go now. Don't know when we will stop again." Everybody but me stumbled out of the car still half-asleep and walked into the store. I decided to stay in the car and try to take a nap. I thought I would sleep now, so I could help Reverend Jackson stay awake while he was driving later.

An attendant came out and started to fill the tank. Inside the store Leroy (as he told me the story later) was leaning on his crutches drinking a soda. He asked the man how much the soda was, and the man said ten cents. Leroy started to comment that he wasn't aware that the price of soda had increased from seven to ten cents, but he decided not to say anything and just pay the man.

About that time, a little black girl came into the store,

and the white men sitting around playing checkers began teasing her. As they teased her, the men watched Leroy's reaction. It was obvious they wanted him to say something, but he didn't.

The young man who was with us walked over to the display counter where Leroy was standing, pointed through the glass, and told the clerk he wanted some peppermint candy. The clerk behind the counter stared at the young man for a second, then with a menacing smirk on his face said, "Did I hear you say you wanted some peppermint candy, boy?"

Still half asleep he yawningly said, "Uh-huh."

The clerk, who was leaning toward the candy, instantly stood upright and said, "Did you say *uh-huh* to me?" And then he used the *n* word and slapped the young man so hard that it turned his whole body around.

The young man had not realized that the clerk was trying to initiate a confrontation from the beginning, and by not saying *yes, sir*, he had given him just the reason he needed to do so.

The clerk then went behind the counter and came up waving a steel hammer and simultaneously yelling to the other white men, "Let's kill them all."

The young man instantly ran out of the store with two of the white men in hot pursuit after him. Leroy, who to this point had just stood and watched, knew it was time to get out of there also. He ran as fast as he could toward the back door. But having only one leg and being on crutches, he was unable to get away. (His leg had been amputated in an accident years prior.) Leroy somehow stumbled to the back door and was about to exit, but an older white man grabbed him and shouted, "I've got this one." He hit Leroy in the face.

Leroy looked at the man and calmly said, "Sir, you know we haven't done anything wrong. We didn't start this! We didn't do anything." The elderly man apologized and reached up and unlatched the screen door. He told Leroy, "Watch out for that bottom step; it's broken. You might fall and hurt yourself." Laughing about it later on, Leroy commented how ironic it was that the man would tell him to be careful of that bottom step after he had just hit him in the mouth.

In the meantime, Reverend Jackson was having major problems at the gas pump. Two men had cornered him and were beating him unmercifully. Blood poured down his face and onto his shirt.

I was lying in the front seat of the car half-asleep. I heard the disturbance and raised up to see what was happening. I couldn't believe my eyes! Why were those white men beating Reverend Jackson? Where was everybody else? What in the world had transpired from the time they went in the store up to now? I couldn't figure it out, but I didn't waste time contemplating it either. I saw one man hit Reverend Jackson in the face and another man pick up an oil drum and crash it down on his back. Reverend Jackson fell down but managed to stagger up again. He swung wildly and somehow succeeded in landing a good blow on one of his attackers. Seeing his friend get hit provoked the man to even more violence. The man with the oil drum hit Reverend Jackson and knocked him down again. But he wouldn't stay down. He was determined to defend his honor that day. I remember it like it happened yesterday. Reverend Jackson had on a light green shirt, but blood covered the front so completely that the only way to tell the color was to look at the back.

I wanted to help but didn't know what to do. Instinctively I wanted to run away from there, but my common sense told me we needed to stay together. But then I noticed everyone else was running. Seemingly they knew what I knew: The time for fighting was over. Fighting wouldn't get us anywhere. If we didn't get out of there, we would all probably be killed.

I thought for a split second about the police. Where were they? We had seen several during the night as we drove down the highway. Unfortunately for us, we were now on our own.

Not having any other choice, I jumped out of the car, looking around and wondering which way to run and where to hide. Across the highway, I saw Reverend Jackson's wife, still clutching her white shawl around her shoulders and staring down at a ditch. She seemed frozen there, uncertain whether she should, or could, jump it.

I heard the white men shouting from behind. I cried out to her, "Girl, you better jump that ditch." From out of nowhere a soda bottle flew through the air and hit Mrs. Jackson on the hip, knocking her into the ditch.

I turned around, and coming directly toward me were two white men, one with a pitchfork and the other with a garden hoe. I didn't wait any longer; it was definitely time to run. And run I did. I began to talk to my feet. I said, like Rochester, "Feet, don't fail me now."

I raced away from that awful place. Forrest Gump had nothing on me that morning. I ran faster than I ever thought I could. From behind I heard a car approaching. Fearing that the white men were coming after me, I forced myself to run even faster. When the car caught up with me, I saw that it was Reverend Jackson and Leroy. Somehow the two had escaped the trouble, and seemingly had gotten away. I breathed a sigh of relief that at least they were okay. But then I saw something else. The two white men from the store were in the backseat hitting and pulling on Reverend Jackson and Leroy. The car slowed up and Leroy hollered to me, "Get in!" But after seeing what was taking place in the car, I yelled back to Leroy, "Never mind, I'm doing better than you!"

Reverend Jackson kept driving while the two men were still beating on him and Leroy from the backseat of the car, and I kept running, oblivious to my surroundings. My only thought was to get away. With one last burst of speed I left behind the men who had been chasing me with the pitchfork and the garden hoe. As I left them in the wind, I turned around and stuck my tongue out at them. That was the little girl coming out of me.

I had no idea where everyone else had gone. The young man, whose sleepy response had evoked such a hostile reaction from the clerk in the store, later told us that he ran into the field across the road from the store. But the white men climbed into a blue Chevrolet truck and drove around and around the field waiting for him to come out. They were determined to catch him. Conceivably, they wanted to kill him.

In retrospect, I know that it was the protective hand of God that did not allow those men to find that young man. It was as though God camouflaged him in the field. Eventually, the young man spotted an old house and ran toward it. In the yard, raking leaves, was a black man who listened to his story, grabbed a gun from the house, and then took him to the state highway patrol office. All of the others were already there. Somehow Leroy and Reverend Jackson had been able to fight the white men off in the backseat of the car and had picked up the other women.

In the meantime, not knowing what was taking place or what buildings I was passing, I ran right past the highway patrol office where, unknown to me, everyone was. I was afraid to stop running because, even though I had distanced myself from the men chasing me, I wasn't sure how far behind they were or if they would get in a car and come after me. So I ran seemingly for hours all the way into Bennettsville, South Carolina. I ended up sitting on a tree stump in a vacant lot, scared and worn-out. I began to wonder what would those men do if they caught me? I knew I wouldn't be able to escape because I was too tired. Where was everyone else? How would my friends know where to find me? Where could I go? I became fearful, but as I prayed, a calmness and peace hovered over me. I knew in my heart that God would never leave me nor forsake me. In my spirit I could hear His Word saying "Lo, I am with you always, even to the ends of the age." I began to say, as did the psalmist David, "Yea, though I walk through the valley of the shadow of death, I will fear no evil; for You are with me." I knew I was going to be all right!

Within moments a highway patrolman pulled into the lot. My friends back at the patrol office had told him what had happened, and he had been searching for me. He took me to where the others were. We stayed at the office while one of the patrolmen went back to the store to question the men who had attacked us. They told the patrolmen that we had come into their store, causing trouble and throwing bottles all over the place.

They lied, and, of course, legal actions were never taken against them. The patrolman explained to us that the magistrate who had jurisdiction over that area had gone fishing for the weekend. They, therefore, could not do anything about what had happened to us. If we wanted to press charges we would have to wait until Monday.

Knowing that regardless of what we did or whom we told justice would not be served, we didn't wait around to press charges. We knew that it was ludicrous for a group of black strangers even to think about filing charges against a group of white residents. There wasn't the slightest possibility of any kind of retribution. As we left, we considered ourselves blessed. Although Reverend Jackson and Leroy were badly beaten and bloody, we were all alive! The best thing to do was to leave that place and put the events behind us. The Lord had spared our lives and that was more than enough.

I relate this story because I have often thought about it. I have often wondered what would have happened if those men had caught me that dreadful morning? Would they have killed me? Would I have ended up like Emmitt Till, mutilated and thrown in some river, only to have my body surface days later? I don't know. But what is certain is that by the grace of God I made it through that ordeal and my life was spared.

I am convinced that God delivered me that day in South Carolina because He had a destiny and divine purpose for me. I will always believe that I escaped because there was a calling upon my life, a God-commission to fulfill, and that was to go into all the world to proclaim the good news of the gospel, not just in spoken words, but also in melodious lyrics. Yes, the melody and the Word! The Lord had chosen me, Baby Shirley Caesar, an underprivileged black girl from where some might consider the wrong side of the tracks in Durham, North Carolina, to be His servant, a vessel of honor. I didn't die that day simply because God said, *Live.*

In many respects that experience is a parable of my being. The course of my life cannot be explained in simple human terms. From the beginning I believe I was destined to fulfill God's purpose and plan for my existence. There is no other explanation. With so much working against me—a semi-invalid mother, a deceased father, low self-esteem resulting from having been called degrading names as a child, and living in a society plagued by racism, sexism, and segregation—I wasn't suppose to make it. I should never have escaped the impoverishment that surrounded me. But by God's great mercy I did. So, here I am—still running, still singing, still preaching.

CHAPTER TWO

The Foundation for Life

THE MELODY

Now, I'm determined to go with Him all the way.
Now, I'm determined to never, never go astray.
I'll go, Lord.
You know, Lord, I'll go with You all the way.
Now, I'm determined to go with Him all the way.
I'm determined to never, never go astray.
I know, Lord; you know, Lord.
I'm going with You all the way.
My mountains are so high, my valleys seem so low.
My burdens press me down so heavy sometimes,
Lord, it seems like I don't know where to go.
Now, I've made up my mind.
I'm going to give You all of my time,
and I'm going with You all the way.
There are times in my life,
times I've been made to cry.

And I just stand around and just wring my hands and ask You
the question, Lord, why.
But into every life some rain just must fall,
And I'm going with You all the way.
—"All the Way"

||||||||||||||||||||||||||||| AND THE WORD |||||||||||||||||||||||||||||

Therefore whoever hears these sayings of Mine, and does them,
I will liken him to a wise man who built his house on the rock.
—Matthew 7:24

——— CHILDHOOD memories are like treasures of the soul. They give you the rare opportunity to look back in time, to see where you were, to understand what made a difference, and to celebrate who you are.

From the very day I was born, I have been a high-energy person. In fact, I came into the world so quickly that my mother didn't have time to make it to the hospital. She went into labor and gave birth to me right at home, at 2209 Chatauqua Street in Durham, North Carolina. I was the tenth of thirteen children; therefore, I learned early the value of sharing, getting along with others, and making the most of only a little. There were five boys—Julius, Leroy, Albert, Cleo, and Solomon—and eight girls—Lucille, Queen Esther, Virginia, Gertrude, Lina, Anne, Joyce, and me. Queen Esther died shortly after birth. With this many children to feed, clothe, and send to school, we had very little extra. A family of this size was typically under-privileged unless there was a rich relative to give assistance; we were not so fortunate. We were totally dependent upon the Lord, and with His help we were determined to make it.

Looking back, I realize that by today's standards people would consider our family quite large. But, in those days, large families were not uncommon. Both my father's family and my mother's family each had fifteen children. Therefore, it seemed only natural to my parents to produce a big family.

Our home was always full of life. The children who had been born close in age moved through the house in shifts—the oldest, the middle, and the youngest. By the time I came along, a few of my brothers and sisters had already grown up and moved out. But there was still plenty of noise and a lot of company. With only one bathroom and three bedrooms to share among the remaining household, you can just imagine the time we had getting ready in the morning and preparing for bed every night.

In those years Durham was a sleepy little southern town where people made a slim living in the tobacco industry or in one of the factories that had recently come South to employ cheap labor. My father, Jim Caesar, a handsome, baldheaded man, made a living as a tobacco worker for Liggett & Myers. He was also a preacher and gospel quartet singer. I don't remember much about him because he died when I was only seven years old. But the memories I do hold are rich, vivid, and lasting.

My father enjoyed singing, singing, and singing. He sang on the way to work and on the way back home. He had a deep voice, but it really wasn't a bass. When he sang, his voice resounded with warmth and strength. I have vague but wonderful memories of him walking home in the evening as the sun was going down, carrying a big sack of potatoes or collard greens over his shoulders, and making a choo-choo sound like a train. Everyone in the community recognized him by that sound. When he walked by, hooting like a train, everyone knew that Jim Caesar was on his way home.

He not only sang going to and from his job, but also during the day while he worked. Friends of my father have said that his singing made their workday go better and that his big voice helped to soothe their frustrations and weariness.

When he wasn't at work for Liggett & Myers, Daddy led a gospel group, the Just Come Four Quartet. When they sang, my, how the Lord did move! Daddy's big voice blessed the people. In those days, churches often hosted "quartet battles," where various quartets gathered for friendly singing competitions. The people came from everywhere and packed the churches. They usually brought food and spent time eating, visiting, and listening to the quartets. The quartet that received the most applause and the loudest shouting from the audience won the battle. It was similar to what happens today on *Showtime at the Apollo*, but in a spiritual sense. More times than not, Daddy's group won. While I don't distinctly recall hearing my father sing on those occasions, the people who did constantly tell me that I sound very much like him and that my energetic ways resemble his. I believe my father gave me both the passion for music and the desire to achieve.

From the earnings with the tobacco industry and the offerings he received from his singing, he provided quite sufficiently for his family. It didn't seem as though we were underprivileged, and in reality we weren't. We certainly did not starve. Many times during the summer, Daddy came home with loads of watermelons for us and for many of our neighbors. The watermelons then cost about twenty-five cents each. That doesn't sound like much money, but in relation to today's economy it was comparable to spending four or five dollars. When he would purchase watermelons, as he often did, all of the children in the community gathered at our house for an ice-cold melon treat. I think that's why I love watermelon to this very day.

My most vivid memory of my father is of him giving me the whipping of my life. I deserved it, but it hurt so badly that I shall never forget it.

As a child I was very daring and mischievous, and I was quite fond of throwing rocks, particularly at streetlights. Streetlights were the most inviting targets. They seemingly called out to me saying, "Break me!" Who was I to say no? I would get a rock, take my aim, throw it directly at the street-light, and miss. The lights were pretty high off the ground. But I would keep trying. One day I threw and threw and threw until, sure enough, I hit one dead-on, a bull's-eye, right in the middle. I heard the most wonderful sound. Pop! Glass smashed to the ground.

But to my immediate sorrow, I discovered I had an eye-witness to my accuracy. Mrs. Carrington, a lady who lived across the street from where the light pole stood, heard the sound of glass breaking and came to her door. I was stand-ing there gazing up into the empty socket of what had once been a streetlight. "Shirley Ann, I'm going to tell your daddy."

Mrs. Carrington was not only my mother's friend but our neighborhood's most unforgettable character. One morn-ing she came to visit. After sitting down, she said to Mama, "Mrs. Caesar, my feet sure do hurt." Looking down at Mrs. Carrington's feet, Mama shook her head in unbelief. "Mrs. Carrington, you have your shoes on the wrong feet." She said, "Oh, I knew it had to be something that was causing that pain in my feet." Whenever she visited she always called for one of us to bring her the newspaper so she could read the obituary column. My mother once asked her, "Mrs. Carrington why do you read the obituary column every day?" She said "Mrs. Caesar, I check the obituary column to make sure that my name is not in there." Oh, by the way, the morning that she did not read it, her name was in the column.

Although she never had children of her own, Mrs. Carrington was a concerned mother figure in the community, and all of the young people respected her. Whenever she saw us doing something that we didn't have any business doing, she would call us into her house, give us a spanking and a nickel, and then send us home.

The evening I broke the streetlight was no exception. Her pronouncement of "Shirley Ann, I'm going to tell your daddy" scared me to death. I knew what would happen if Daddy found out! He would "wear me out." My eyes quickly filled with tears, and I started pleading with Mrs. Carrington. "Please, please don't tell."

Ignoring my tears and my appeal, she told me to come inside her house. Afraid to say no, I did what she said. As I knew she would, she spanked me. That's right. She spanked me herself for what I had done. Contrary to some cynical critics, it does take a village to raise a child, and Mrs. Carrington did her part to help raise me.

To be honest, while she was spanking me, she really was not hurting me. Her lashes were more like love taps, especially if you compared them to my father's whippings. However, in spite of the love taps, hearing my cries, you would have thought she was killing me. In fact, I am surprised that the entire neighborhood didn't come to my rescue.

After she finished whipping me, true to character, Mrs. Carrington gave me a nickel. To me, that seemed like a lot of money. It was almost worth getting the whipping. Before leaving, I again pleaded with Mrs. Carrington. "Please don't tell my daddy." As I left her house, I thought the matter was settled. I figured that, as hard and as loud as I had cried, she would be convinced that her punishment was enough. Surely, she wouldn't whip me and tell Daddy too.

But I guess I had not cried hard enough. Or maybe she felt she had not spanked me enough. When I got home, I went into the kitchen, stretched out on the floor, and began reading a comic book.

My father got off work about 5:00. From work he usually stopped by his garden to dig potatoes or pick some other vegetable to bring home. This particular evening, with a sack of potatoes on his shoulders, Daddy walked into the house at the exact time the telephone was ringing. It was Mrs. Carrington. After speaking with her, he immediately hung the phone up and dropped his sack of potatoes. I could tell by the look in his eyes that something was wrong.

Without a word he walked over to where I was and lifted me off the floor, just as he had that sack of potatoes, carried me into the back room, and gave me a good whipping. In yesterday's vernacular, he gave me a what for. The man tore me up. As the disciplinarian, my father simply did not tolerate disobedience. Although he was firm with me, he was even more harsh with my brothers. He had very little patience with their shenanigans. I think he really wanted to do everything he could to keep them out of trouble. There were times when he would whip the boys to the extent that Mama would have to go into the room and say, "That's enough, Jim. I mean that's enough." He would immediately stop.

I know that in this twenty-first century spanking children has almost become obsolete; however, I can't help but think that all of my mother's children turned out for the better because of the discipline we received. It is not that my father abused us, but he did try to live out the meaning of the Scripture that says, "Spare the rod and spoil the child."

As a child, I never forgot that whipping I received from

my father for breaking out the streetlight, and I never forgot the spanking Mrs. Carrington gave me or the fact that she had told on me. And in my own mischievous way, I was determined to get even with her.

I must have been about eight years old when Mrs. Carrington came again to visit Mama. As she seated herself in the living room, she called to me. "Gal, go in there and get me some water." Instead of going to the kitchen sink to get the water, I reached for a glass, took it into the bathroom, flushed the commode, placed the glass against the interior of the commode, and allowed the water to fill the glass. Graciously, I handed the glass to Mrs. Carrington. Taking a swallow, she exclaimed: "Oh, that was good and cold. Bring me some more." And that is exactly what I did. (Oh, how I thank God for forgiving us even of our childish sins.)

Looking back on that whipping I received from Daddy, I can say for a certainty that I deserved it. He spanked me because he wanted to teach me respect for property, respect for the law, and respect for others. To my deepest sorrow, however, he died the very next morning around 2:00 A.M. I guess that is why that whipping stands in the forefront of my mind above all others.

I remember the funeral attendants brought Daddy's body to our house for the wake. Of course this is not the custom today, but it was in those days. Friends and neighbors brought food to my mother and her children. They would hug us and pray, reminding us that Daddy had gone to heaven to be with the Lord.

On the day of the funeral, the minister, Reverend Lawson, came to our house to pray with the family and to accompany us to the church. All of the family filed out of the house and gathered in cars and limousines. I remember hiding in a closet because I didn't want to go to the funeral. It was the first time

I had ever seen a dead body, and it frightened me. The night before as I stood on my tiptoes looking at my father lying in his coffin, I remembered how strong and alive he had been. I remembered his singing, his laughter, and his praying. Now he lay so silent, so still, and so cold. As I hid in that closet, I could hear my oldest sister, Lucille, asking, "Where is Shirley Ann?" My brother Leroy searched the house until he found me and dragged me out of the house, screaming, crying, and hollering. Lucille called out to me, saying "Come here, Shirley, I have something for you." When I was within arm's reach, she picked me up, placed me in the limousine, and closed the door. Slowly, we drove away. And yes, I continued to holler as though someone was killing me. I just didn't want to go.

I don't remember much about the funeral, just that they buried Daddy in a light blue, clothlike coffin. We couldn't afford anything better. My dad had not accumulated much monetary wealth, but he was rich in love and admiration. People came in great numbers to pay their last respects. His funeral must have been one of the largest in the history of Durham.

My father's sudden death meant intense economic hardship for the family. My mother, who was a semi-invalid, did her very best to provide for us. Although physically challenged, she was by no means a weak lady. But her handicapped foot made it impossible for her to work on a full-time job. Thankfully, as my brothers and sisters grew older they got jobs to help supplement our income. They brought all the income they earned home to Mama, and she added it to the support we received from the government. Through careful management and strict budgeting, she was able to keep a roof over our heads, clothes on our backs, and food on the table.

With Daddy gone, we were also faced with the possibility

of separation. A few of my aunts and uncles wanted to adopt some of us to help lessen the financial strain on Mama. Uncle Wesley wanted to adopt me, and Aunt Julia wanted to adopt my sister Anne. But my mother declared, "I might not have much, but with the little that I do have, I am going to keep all of my children together, by the grace of God."

There were those who felt that my mother was being overly courageous. To give away two or three of us would have certainly lightened the load. One lady in particular, Mother Elizabeth Jones, who lived next door to us and often took me to sing at her church in Goshen, North Carolina, asked Mama if she could adopt me. But my mother would not hear of it. She continuously said no. "It wouldn't please your father," she told us. "And it doesn't please me either. God gave me all of my children, and I'm not giving you away to anybody."

We struggled, but at least we struggled together as a family. For a time, things even got worse. Shortly after Daddy died, the house that we were renting was purchased right from under us. Mr. Markham, who was supposed to have been my father's best friend, purchased the property. We had lived in that house all of my life. In fact, most of my brothers and sisters and I were born right there. Now, we were being forced to leave. The saddest thing about it was that we didn't have anywhere else to go. All I could think of was that my father had lived a good Christian life and had been a good husband and father. Now that he was gone, why was this happening to his family? Mama just did not understand how Mr. Markham could do such an underhanded thing to the family of his deceased best friend. For a while we were quite frightened and Mama didn't know what to do. But, true to his promise, God made a way out of no way.

Mr. Scarborough, the funeral director who handled my

father's arrangements, heard about our predicament and called my mother to tell her that he had just the house for us. But when he told her the location of the house, Mama said that the area was too bad and she was not taking her children there. I'm sure Mama must have been talking to a higher power because to turn down a place to live when we didn't have anyplace to go seemed totally illogical. Mr. Scarborough continuously called, and Mama repeatedly said no.

Then one day, Mr. Carver, our life insurance agent, came by to collect the monthly premium. He said to Mama, "Mrs. Caesar, I understand that you are going to have to move. I have a house over on Simmons Street that I can sell you for four thousand dollars." We all went over to look at the house. It was a white frame house with a porch running along the front with a wood railing. The paint was faded and peeling. There were six rooms, indoor plumbing, and electricity, but no bathtub. There were three bedrooms, one for Mama, one for me and my sisters, and one for my brothers. My mother felt that this house would be adequate for our family. Another plus was that it was located in a safe, quiet neighborhood. Also, Oak Grove Free Will Baptist Church was located one block away from the house, so we would never have an excuse for not attending church.

We loaded everything that we owned and moved to our new house. Eight of us lived there: my mother and I; my three sisters—Anne, Joyce, and Lina; my two brothers—Cleo and Solomon; and a nephew—Harold. For a while everything was fine, but one day, black clouds began to form, the sky turned very dark, and a heavy rain began to fall. We understood then why Mr. Carver had this house available. It was located at the bottom of a hill, and sat very low to the ground with no underpinnings. Consequently, when it rained all of the water would run down the hill toward our house. When it reached the bottom, we got flooded because of the poor drainage system. After the rain stopped, we would wash everything down, clean it up, and keep on going.

Even with that big problem, the Lord was with us in that house. Wonderful neighbors surrounded us. The Dixons, who lived directly across the street, had children, Dorothy, Edna, and Edward, who were our playmates. Mrs. Myrtle lived next door to us, and that was very good for my brothers and me because whenever she needed someone to go to the store or run an errand or just keep her wood box supplied, she would call on us. That was twenty-five to fifty cents I could always count on, and please believe me, Mama could always use any extra change that was brought in.

Amazingly, we didn't really think about the fact that we were not well off. Maybe that was because almost everyone in our community lived by the same standards. We resided in the same type of house, we shopped for our clothing at the same stores, and all of the children played in the same pot-holed, muddy streets. Occasionally, we would go to the Hillside School Park to play ball and other games. Everyone in our community worked hard to make a living. Since we were all of the same socioeconomic class, no one paid any attention to what one family had or did not have. However, there is one thing we all did: We supported one another and shared whatever resources we had. If anyone needed a ride to work or just needed to borrow an egg or a cup of sugar, all they had to do was ask a neighbor and the request was granted.

In many ways we had an abundance, maybe even more than we have today—not financially, of course, but socially. We had a community, a real neighborhood, an extended family where people looked out for each other. We lived among people who helped to keep us on the straight and narrow. If you got into mischief, the neighbors made sure that your parents knew about it. As a young girl, I disliked the adults who told on my friends and me, but now I realize that they—including Mrs. Carrington—were instrumental in holding our neighborhoods together. Crime and juvenile delinquency were almost nonexistent.

Of all the factors that held our neighborhood and our lives together, none was more influential than the church. From the very beginning, I was immersed in the gospel tradition, in both my family and church. We prayed together, worshiped together, and lived out our Christian beliefs in our daily lives. The church was so central to my upbringing that I can't recall participating in very many activities that were not religious in nature. My spare time was primarily spent in church.

I grew up in the Pentecostal Church, which is noted for its expressive praise and worship unto God. To say the least, we didn't hold back when it came to glorifying and magnifying the God of our salvation. We believed in praising the Lord hard and long. Many times our Sunday worship would last all day. After our morning service we would take a break to eat and go right into an afternoon worship hour. Then at 6:00, YPHA (Young People's Holiness Association) would convene. During this time the youth of the church would engage in Bible study, preaching, and singing. At 8:00 there would be an evening evangelistic service. No one complained about being in church all day long; we were just happy to be in the presence of the Lord. That was the depth of our devotion.

Fisher Memorial United Holy Church in Durham was the first church that I can remember attending. Then, when I was about eight or nine years old, my family moved to East Durham, and we began attending the Mount Calvary Holy Church. This little church was not very appealing to the eyes inside or out. Paint peeled from the walls, and the thin wooden floor was filled with cracks. Looking down through those cracks, I could see rabbits and chickens running around underneath the floor. The roof leaked so badly that often we had to put up our umbrellas when it rained to keep the drops from hitting us on the head. In the winter, we filled the pot-bellied stove with wood to warm the sanctuary. In spite of these dilapidated conditions, the Lord's presence was always in the midst of our services. We had more joy in those primitive conditions than many people experience in most cathedrals today.

I grew up in that church under the powerful ministry of Bishop Frizelle Yelverton. I remember how I looked forward to hearing him preach week after week. He preached anointed, inspired messages of salvation and deliverance, and he was considered one of the leading ministers in the city. Bishop Yelverton's preaching seemed to convict every listener. His weekly radio broadcast was heard in nearly every home in the surrounding areas. As a result of his preaching and teaching, my knowledge of God increased and I grew spiritually. He made it clear that soul salvation was a serious matter and that children were not exempt. We were all encouraged to seek a personal relationship with the Lord. One of the first lessons we were taught was to reverence the house of the Lord. Children then did not have as much freedom to roam as they do today. Parents would not allow them to run up and down the aisles, chew gum, play with the bulletins, and go to the bathroom every five minutes. While in church we sat like stones, scared that we would get a good spanking from one of the mothers of the church if we dared to move. Parents did not believe in sparing the rod. I learned early in life that church was serious business.

However, like most children, before I actually had a

personal encounter with Jesus, I would imitate the saints. I did not do so in a mean or disrespectful manner, but playfully. I learned to dance and shout just like them. I pretended to be Sister Jones or Sister Bertha. I would throw my head back in the air, wave my handkerchief, and shake as if the Holy Spirit had touched me.

Despite my playing, the church taught me the basics of my faith. The truths I learned there became the foundation of my life and of my music. The elders and the preachers taught me by precept and example. (Later, when the Lord called me to preach the gospel, I discovered that my days in that little frail church had helped prepare me for God's mighty work.) Even today in my own ministry I feel close to the elders of that church. Often, I find myself trying to pass on to a new generation the values I gained from those early Christians.

The church played a key role not only in preparing me for the proclamation of the Word but also for the melody of the Word. I trace my desire to sing and my first musical influences back to my brothers and sisters and the choir members who led songs in weekly worship services. I suppose, had it not been for my singing gospel songs in the church along with my brothers and sisters, there is a great possibility that I may have ended up singing another genre of music.

Not only did the church play a great role in my singing ministry, but it also gave me the spiritual reservoir that I yet draw from today. I honestly believe that my stability in the Lord Jesus is attributable to all of the sound teaching and preaching I received as a child.

However, like most children, I didn't always want to hear instruction or receive correction. There were times when I even rebelled against going to church. At the age of twelve, I was a bit sassy. I wasn't cruel, but I was prone to occasional mischief. I got into arguments with my brothers and sisters, went outside to play when Mama told me to do chores, did not pay attention as much as I should have while in church, and did not want to do my homework.

The worst of my waywardness occurred because I had an incredible love for Popsicles—those juicy, fruity, cold sticks of frozen ice. I had a habit of stopping by a store on the way home from school. Like many other kids, I did not have much money, so I would stand around in the store looking and talking with my friends, imagining that I could buy whatever I wanted. One day, I went beyond imagining. I did something about what I wanted. I took something that was not mine.

Once the owner of the store turned his back, I reached down into the freezer and grabbed a handful of those delightful, tasty treats. Before he turned back around, I stuffed them under my coat and walked out.

Wanting to keep what I had done a secret and not wanting to share the Popsicles with any of the other kids, I walked home slowly, taking the longest route through an old graveyard. That way I would not run into anybody. Step by step I walked and ate each and every single one of those Popsicles—grape, orange, lemon, and banana. The juice dripped down my chin and onto my fingers and my dress. I didn't care. Nothing had ever tasted quite so good.

Having finished the Popsicles, I hastened home, thinking I had gotten away with my wrongdoing. But by the time I reached home and walked onto the porch, word of what I had done had somehow reached Mama. "Girl, get in here," she yelled out to me.

Pretending to be innocent, I opened the door and walked into the house. "What's wrong?" I asked.

Mama said, "I hear you've been stealing."

"Me?" I replied, trying to look shocked. "I didn't steal anything, Mama."

"Stick out your tongue," she said, her voice stern.

Meekly, I obeyed. My tongue had Popsicle stains all over it.

"Now look at your dress."

Though I hated to do it, I stared down and saw all the stains. I had sticky hands too. I had done a bad thing, and Mama knew it.

"I'm going to whip you for lying and stealing," Mama said. "Now, come to me like you came into the world."

I knew what that meant. She wanted me to come to her naked. I was due for a whipping like I would never forget. Mama had a stern sense of right and wrong, and I had crossed the line. After that whipping, I never stole another Popsicle—or anything else, for that matter.

I had a desire to do better. Although I did not really think about it at the time, my lying and stealing could have led to real trouble in later life. If the Lord had not saved me, I don't know how I would have ended up.

The single most important event of my life happened at age twelve. I was in the backyard with my brother Solomon and my sister Anne. We were getting ready to play church. Solomon had a Bible in his hand and a handkerchief to wipe his face as he had seen other preachers do as they preached and sweated. We also had an empty soda case that served as his podium.

Solomon began playing the role of the preacher. He was doing a wonderful job of it too. He stood behind the pulpit, shouting, preaching, exhorting, and convicting. Wanting us to get involved, he waved his arms and shouted, "Jump up and shout *Jesus* three times."

Anne and I jumped up and shouted, "Jesus."

The instant we hit the ground, we jumped a second time and shouted again, "Jesus."

As I jumped to my feet the third time, the most amazing thing happened. Right there in the backyard, my skinny little body suspended in midair, the word *Jesus* hanging on my lips, the power of the Holy Ghost exploded within me. I think that is why today I love to sing the name Jesus. As I looked up toward heaven, I felt the powerful presence of the Lord. It was as if the hand of God reached down and touched me. I felt warm and tingly all over, energized by a bolt of holy electricity.

By the time I landed on the ground, tears were streaming down my cheeks. As the prophet Jeremiah had declared, it was just like "fire shut up in my bones." I raised my face toward the sun, and it was as though God stood right beside me.

Surprised by my tears and my behavior, Anne ran into the house, calling Mama. We had already been warned not to play church. Anne kept shouting, "Mama, come out here. Shirley is playing with the Lord again." She led Mama to the window and pointed out to me. "Look at her," she said.

Slowly, Mama made her way to the backdoor. She opened the screen and leaned out. For several seconds, she stood and watched me, a puzzled look on her face. Then she smiled and turned back to Anne and said, "Shirley ain't playing this time."

I will always remember that day. As Mama put it, I wasn't playing that time. The Lord had reached down His blessed hand and touched me from the top of my head to the tip of my toes. From that day forward, I have known that Jesus is Lord, and I have tried to reflect this reality in my life and music.

After my conversion, my music ministry (which had already begun and which will be discussed in detail in the next chapter) became even busier. I traveled extensively and became more and more in demand to minister in churches and render concerts.

I loved it all. At the same time, however, my music ministry kept me awfully preoccupied. Maybe I grew up too fast. The years skipped by in a hurry, and I don't remember having time just to play and be a little girl. It seemed as though I was always headed to catch a bus to perform a concert at some church out of town. I did not stop to think much about all of this then. At the time, all I wanted to do was to sing and to help provide for my mother and family.

As I became even busier singing, I also became more earnest about witnessing to other people. Everywhere I went, I poured myself into testifying. At school and in the neighborhood, I took every opportunity to tell someone else about Jesus. I was more zealous in those days than I was considerate; I never even thought about the fact that some people might have been won to Jesus with a softer, gentler approach. I just plowed straight ahead, telling persons to get right with God.

Although I didn't realize it at the time, many of my fellow students at school were laughing at me. Had I known, I still would not have cared. I had a burning passion to tell people about Jesus. Many people who laughed at me then now call on me to pray for them. They often express their pride in knowing me. They see me as someone who has "stickability" because I have managed, by the grace of God, to stick to what I believe all these years.

Even before my actual anointing to preach, I sensed that God wanted me to preach as well as to sing. I saw my ministry as twofold. The Lord called me to the melody of song and the ministry of the Word; He called me to use music to preach. Anyone who has been to any of my group's concerts or who has attended my church knows this is what I do: I sing a sermon and I preach a song. I'm a singing evangelist.

My actual call to the gospel ministry happened in 1957,

five years after my salvation. Vividly, I remember sitting in a class at North Carolina Central University taking a typing test. It was the year after my high school graduation, and I had begun to take some college courses. I was not exactly sure just what the Lord had in store for me. I knew I wanted to further my education, but I also wanted to sing full time. I didn't have much money to advance my education, but I tried my best to raise enough money to continue my studies.

But right in the middle of that typing test, I heard the voice of the Lord. It wasn't exactly what most folks think of as a spiritual moment. It did not occur while I was in church. It did not happen while I read the Bible or prayed. It did not even happen while I was singing. It happened right there in a typing class.

Another girl was seated beside me. When I heard the voice, initially I thought she had asked me something. I leaned over and said, "What did you say?"

She looked up from her typing and stared at me. "I didn't say anything," she remarked, and then returned to her work.

Becoming a little confused, I tried to focus again on my test. I did not feel well, however, so after the test I went straight home. My head felt kind of woozy, and I fell across my bed.

As I was lying there, trying to feel better, I again heard the voice. This time it was more pronounced, and the reality hit me. "God was trying to tell me something." I listened closer and the words came quite clear to me. *Behold I have called you, and I have ordained you from your mother's womb to preach the gospel.*

These were the words the Lord spoke to Jeremiah, the prophet who was called to preach salvation to Israel. I did not fully understand what those words meant at that moment, but I interpreted them to mean God was calling me to preach as well as to sing. I did not feel torn to choose between the two, and I really can't say which I prefer. As I see it, they go together. Why should one be regarded as more important than the other? For me, it's a matter of using every gift the Lord has given me to make His ways known to the world.

On the day following that typing class, the Lord laid upon me the mantle of my dad to sing and the mantle of my pastor, Bishop Frizelle Yelverton, to preach. From then forward, I labored to do both, even though I had no idea how. But it was irrelevant that I didn't know, because the Lord did, and I was confident that He would lead and guide me. All I had to do was stay faithful, and God would work it out.

To my amazement, because I had willingly submitted to His will, God rewarded my diligence and my faithfulness. My ministry began to soar to horizons I had never imagined. I became living proof of Jesus' words: "You have been faithful over few things, now I will make you ruler over many things."

CHAPTER THREE

Born to Sing

THE MELODY

It's been worth having the Lord in my life
I'm satisfied just living for Jesus Christ
It's been worth having the Lord in my life
I don't know what I would do without the Lord

Every day gets sweeter walking with the Savior
I get all excited every time I talk with Him, with Him
You haven't lived until you've lived for Christ
In Him there is security in a world of uncertainty
We need Jesus

It was the Grace of God
that brought me down through the years
It was the Grace of God
that took away all of my fears

It's been worth having the Lord in my life
I don't know what I would do without the Lord
—"It's Been Worth Having the Lord in My Life"

﹏﹏﹏﹏﹏﹏﹏AND THE WORD﹏﹏﹏﹏﹏﹏﹏

It is good to give thanks to the LORD,
And to sing praises to Your name, O Most High;
To declare Your lovingkindness in the morning,
And Your faithfulness every night.
On an instrument of ten strings,
On the lute,
And on the harp,
With harmonious sound.
—Psalm 92:1–3

——— GOSPEL music has always been a viable part of my life. It was the first music I heard as an infant, and the only music that was sung in our household. My mother could always be heard humming a song of praise or singing a hymn as she joyfully accomplished her daily tasks. My father also loved gospel music with a passion. He sang at home, on his way to work, at work, and on his way home from work. The neighbors always heard Big Jim Caesar's huge voice coming down the street singing praises to God. Throughout the Carolinas and southern states, he was noted for his anointed and energetic style of singing. When he and his group, the Just Come Four Quartet, would sing at a church, I'm told he could electrify and magnetize an audience like no one else could. My father passed this legacy down to each and every one of his children. As far back as I can remember, I was singing gospel music. Often the youngest of the children in our family—Joyce, Anne, Solomon, and I—would sing together. When friends or family gathered at our house, they always wanted to hear us sing.

Everyone would gather around our old, battered piano, and we would sing our favorite tunes, tunes such as "Nearer My God to Thee," "I Know the Lord Will Make a Way Somehow," and "I've Heard of a City Called Heaven." Often my brother Leroy played the piano. Sometimes I tried to pluck out the tune. But we would sing until the very presence of the Lord would saturate that room. It was as though heaven and earth were coming together.

Like my father, my life evolved around gospel music. I would rather sing than eat. I would rather sing than go outside and play. I recall an incident when my sister Anne invited a group of her friends to our house for a Halloween party. When they arrived I went to the piano and started playing and singing. Before too long, most of her friends had joined me around the piano. We were all singing gospel songs and having a good time.

Unintentionally, I had drawn all of Anne's friends away from her party, and she was quite upset. She ran to Mama and said, "Shirley has taken all of my friends away."

Mama told her, "Don't be angry with her. Just go back in there and sing too." And that's what she did, and needless to say we turned that Halloween party into church.

Apart from home, the church was the primary medium through which I was exposed to gospel music. In our family, attending church was not an option—it was an obligation. If you lived in our household, you went to church mid-week and all day Sunday, including Sunday school. My mother contended that if you went to public school Monday through Friday, you were certainly getting up to go to God's school on Sunday morning.

In our church we had a junior and senior choir, and in each service one of the choirs sang. Tuesday nights were junior church night, and I particularly enjoyed these services, because

I knew I would have the opportunity to sing at church, either in the choir or as a soloist, possibly both. From time to time, the junior choir and myself were also given the opportunity to sing at our Wednesday night prayer meetings and our Friday night evangelistic services. When our junior choir sang I made sure my contralto voice was heard loud and clear. When I sang as a soloist I sang as though my very life depended on the projection of that song.

When the senior choir sang one of my gospel favorites, I would close my eyes and sing along with them. When the congregation sang a hymn, I raised my voice the loudest. I loved singing God's music, and I was so thankful that He had blessed me with a voice to sing glory unto Him. Like my father, wherever I went or whatever I did, I was always singing. When I played in the school yard, I sang. When I walked to school, I sang. When I did my chores at home, I sang. From the time I was born, it seemed as if music was in my spirit, and nothing gave me greater joy than singing gospel music.

Often my mother assigned my sister Anne and me the task of washing and drying the dishes. The sink was beneath the kitchen window, through which you could see our back-yard. During the summer months we kept the window open to try to attract a cool breeze. While we washed dishes, Anne and I would harmonize a song to make the chore more pleasant. We didn't care that the window was open; we sang at the top of our voices.

The people in the neighborhood heard us singing night after night. Frequently, the next day they would tell Anne and me how much they enjoyed our singing. With that sense of encouragement fueling my desire to sing, I sang even more. As more and more people became aware of my ability to sing, I began receiving invitations to sing at churches, at schools, and at various other functions. From that point, my gospel singing career began to develop, gradually at first, but then with a sense of inevitability it began to flourish. Seemingly, it sprang from the ground, like a wildflower, no one really expecting it or trying to make it happen. I know now that it was all part of God's divine plan for my life.

Shortly afterward, I began singing with a choir, the Charity Singers of Durham, North Carolina. As Baby Shirley Caesar, I became their mascot. I was the little girl with the enormous voice who would come to the church podium, lead one or two songs with the choir, and then do what most young children do in church at that age: I fell asleep while the preacher delivered the sermon.

Concurrently, while singing with the Charity Singers, members of my family and I formed our own gospel group, which consisted of two of my sisters, Anne and Joyce, our cousin Esther, and occasionally my brother Solomon. One song I especially liked to sing was one recorded by the Angelic Gospel Singers that said, "Some day, I'm going to see my Lord. Walk around heaven and spread the news. Put on my shiny, golden shoes. When my Savior calls me home."

When I wasn't singing with the Charity Singers, or my sisters and cousin, I was singing with my brother's group. All I wanted was the opportunity to sing God's praises. Whenever or however the opportunity presented itself, I took advantage of it. I recall once while singing in Lynchburg, Virginia, with my brother's group that I wanted to sing a song his group didn't know. The song, "I'm Sending Up My Timber Every Day," was a Mahalia Jackson recording, and one of my favorites. My brother Leroy told me since his group didn't know it I would have to sing it a cappella. Again, the opportunity to sing had arisen, and I wasn't going to let it pass. So I sang a cappella. I'm sure the Lord looking from heaven decided to reward my willingness and boldness, because the very presence of the Holy Spirit could be felt throughout the sanctuary. The congregation applauded and applauded, while shouting for me to sing again. Later, Leroy jokingly told me, "I don't think I want to take you to sing with us again. Once they hear you, they don't want to hear us."

Over a short span of time, my music ministry expanded. People beyond our little circuit began inviting me to assist in their ministry. A number of churches began asking me to lead their devotional services.

My pastor, Bishop Yelverton, began taking me with him when he was called to preach in other churches. Before he preached, I would sing. Many times the anointing of the Holy Spirit would infiltrate the services so strongly that it wouldn't be necessary for Bishop Yelverton to preach. I traveled with him from church to church, from town to town. I didn't know a lot about the dynamics of music, but I did know I enjoyed singing. And I sang with every ounce of energy and fervency I could generate from within the depths of my soul. Many times when I sang, people would stand me on a wooden box so I could be seen. I found it difficult to stay on that box because even then I loved to move among the audience while singing. I loved to walk the aisles and interact with the people. I loved to sing in transition, and standing on that box was too confining.

By the time I was thirteen, I was actually a member of a very popular gospel group, Thelma Bumpass and the Royalettes. Thelma, a blind lady, sang lead along with her sister, Augusta. We traveled from town to town and church to church throughout North and South Carolina, and as far north as Washington, D.C. I remained with the Royalettes for approximately two years.

In those years, churches all over the South had an unstructured but effective method of networking. Pastors and members told others about singers and preachers that they should invite to minister in their churches. Groups like the Dixie Hummingbirds, the Gospel Harmonettes, the Soul Stirrers, the Five Blind Boys, and the sensational Nightingales were the most noted in the network. Among individual singers, the great Mahalia Jackson and the Reverend James Cleveland were the most sought after. Everyone tried to emulate them.

Traveling with Leroy Johnson, we were a part of that network. We were not among the most celebrated groups, but the network proved effective for us. Inevitably, even after I no longer traveled as a team with Leroy Johnson, my name was still a part of the gospel network.

As a child, whenever I traveled my mother always took precautions for my safety and always ensured that I didn't get lonely. She insisted that a family member always accompanied whomever I was traveling with. Of course, I loved singing and traveling too much to get lonely. The hectic pace we kept up also kept me from ever getting lonely. It was always a rush, rush, rush schedule. We often sang at one church on Sunday morning, another in the afternoon, and a third that night. From there we traveled home so I could be in school Monday. Often I didn't get home until 2:00 or 3:00 in the morning.

Totally exhausted from my weekend of travels, I spent a lot of Mondays with my eyes half-closed in school. The principal of the school and several of my teachers complained to Mama, telling her I needed to stop traveling on weekends so I could study and get more rest. But my schedule didn't change. I didn't want to stop traveling and singing gospel. But most important, my father was deceased, and my mother needed the money I received from singing on weekends. Eventually, my teachers became more supportive. They knew my family's plight. And I think they finally began to realize that singing gospel music was my destiny in life.

One teacher in particular was very supportive. Mr. Charlie Roach, my sixth-grade teacher, would often allow me to leave class early on Fridays in order to catch an earlier bus to where I was scheduled to sing that weekend.

I regret that I didn't completely apply myself academically in school. My grades didn't bespeak my scholastic aptitude. Both Mama and I knew I could do better. Even though my GPA (grade point average) was high enough for me to enter directly into a four-year college institution (as opposed to going to junior college after high school graduation), we always knew I had not reached my full academic potential during the years I was traveling and singing as Baby Shirley Caesar. I always felt torn between school and singing. If I had to do it all over again, I honestly don't know what I would do. But I do know that "All things work together for good to those who love God." My education was delayed but not denied.

Singing gospel music was always my first love. It was my way of giving praise to God and telling others about Him. Even at the tender age of eight years old, my mother had taught me so much about Jesus that I felt He was my best friend. Within my heart there was always a keen desire to please Him. And I wanted others to share my enthusiasm about the Lord. I've always felt that one of the best ways to tell others of God's love, His grace and mercy, was through singing gospel music.

Singing gospel music also granted me the privilege of helping my mother with the finances needed to raise twelve children. Because I knew how much Mama needed the money, I was determined to bring every dime back to her. Sometimes, while sitting in the bus station on my way home from singing,

I would be hungry, but I wouldn't spend any of the money on a hamburger or soda because I knew Mama needed it at home. I was very determined to take care of my mother. She had made many sacrifices for her children, and I didn't mind sacrificing for her and my brothers and sisters. I was determined that nothing would stop me from caring for my mother. Early in my singing career, before I sang with Leroy Johnson, I was traveling with a preacher named Reverend Jones. We had traveled for one week together, going from church to church. He preached and I sang. As was the custom, a free-will offering was collected for us at the end of the services.

At the end of the week when it was time to be paid, I went to Reverend Jones expecting him to give me my share of the offering.

He smiled and placed two quarters in my hand. He patted me on the head and told me to go buy myself an ice-cream cone. I looked down at those two quarters and thought within myself, I can't take only fifty cents home to Mama. Reverend Jones said, "The Lord is going to bless you."

Even though I knew the Lord would surely bless me, before I realized it I had blurted out, "My blessing is in your pocket."

He laughed a bit nervously, then pushed my hand away and said, "Don't sass me, girl."

I never received more than fifty cents from him that day, and I didn't like it when I had to go home with such a small amount to give Mama. But I have to confess, one Halloween night shortly after that incident, my friends and I sneaked up on Reverend Jones's front porch and took the chairs he had sitting out there. We used those chairs to climb his pear tree and take all of his pears. I took those pears home, and Mama, not knowing where I had gotten them, made pear preserves and pear pies. Reverend Jones never paid me my money, but indirectly he helped me take care of Mama, because we certainly enjoyed those preserves and pies. After that, I didn't sing with him any more.

By the time I was thirteen, the Lord had blessed Baby Shirley Caesar to sing in scores of churches across the South. Although I had no idea then that the Lord would anoint my ministry the way He has, I was always aware that God wanted to use my life in a unique way.

Looking back, I plainly see the hand of God leading my life. So many things could have happened to me. I could have fallen into divers temptations. My life could have taken many detours. I could have strayed away from the Lord. But for the grace of God, I could have become an alcoholic, a drug addict, or an unwed mother. So many things could have happened, but thanks be to God, they didn't. The power of the Holy Spirit threw a protective shield of spiritual armor around me and gave me strength to resist temptation.

I shall never forget the night I received the baptism of the Holy Spirit. Earlier that day, while playing church in our backyard with my brother and sister, the Holy Spirit had transformed our playtime into a genuine spiritual experience, and I felt the power of God move *on* me. But the night God baptized me in His Holy Spirit, I felt the power of God not only move on me but also move *in* me. It was an experience that changed my life forever.

For two weeks, Pastor Dorothy Elam Keith had been in revival at our church. And, of course, I attended every night. In our family, the only reason you weren't at church every time the door opened was that something catastrophic had occurred to prevent you from being there. This was Tuesday night of the second week of the revival, Valentine's Day. I was sitting in the back of the church, still feeling exhilarated from my backyard experience with the Lord. One of the mothers of the church, Mother Mildred Reid, stood up to sing. I remember the song as if it were yesterday, "In shady green pastures, so rich and so sweet, God leads his dear children along; where the water's cool flow bathes the weary one's feet, God leads his dear children along. Some through the waters, some through the flood, some through the fires, but all through the blood."

That song ushered in the presence of the Lord, and without warning that same overwhelming presence of Jesus I had felt earlier moved on me again. With my spiritual ears I heard a knock at the door of my heart, and I ran to the window of my soul and looked out. With my spiritual eyes I saw Jesus standing there saying, "Behold, I stand at the door and knock. If anyone hears My voice and opens the door, I will come in to him and will dine with him, and he with Me." I believe Jesus was saying, "I want to come in, Shirley, and have the last meal of the day with you." I jumped up and ran to the altar. I fell on my face before the Lord. It was that Valentine's night when the Lord totally changed my life. There is a difference in the power of God moving on you and the power of God moving in you. That night I submitted my will to God's will. I gave Him complete control of my life. From that night forward I only wanted to live according to His divine will for my life. I believe the Holy Spirit indwelt me that night, but I wanted the manifestation of that indwelling to be evidenced in my life according to Acts 2:4, "And they were all filled with the Holy Spirit and began to speak with other tongues, as the Spirit gave them utterance."

Two nights later, on my way to church, I felt a sudden impulse to visit Mother House. While sitting and talking to her, she said, "Shirley, you can be filled with the Holy Ghost before you get to church tonight."

I told her I wanted that more than anything else in the world.

It may sound unusual now, but no sooner than I spoke those words the power of God leveled me. There I lay on my back, my hands reaching toward the heavens. Mother House stood over me and prayed. I prayed also, saying, "Lord Jesus, come into my heart, and fill me with Your Holy Spirit."

I was baptized in the Holy Spirit, and I began to speak in a heavenly language. I'll never forget that night. I felt that the Lord had given me the power to withstand any temptation that came my way, the courage to say no to sin and evil, the strength to walk through the fiery furnaces of life, and a greater desire to tell others about Jesus in melody and in Word. I wanted to perpetuate Acts 1:8 in my life, "But you shall receive power when the Holy Spirit has come upon you; and you shall be witnesses to Me in Jerusalem, and in all Judea and Samaria, and to the end of the earth."

With the fullness of Christ in my life, I was ready for the next step in my life's journey for the Lord. Before I tell you about that journey, let me tell you about the one who, next to the Lord, made it all possible.

CHAPTER FOUR

I Remember Mama

‖‖‖‖‖‖‖‖‖‖‖‖‖‖‖‖‖‖‖‖‖‖‖ THE MELODY ‖‖‖‖‖‖‖‖‖‖‖‖‖‖‖‖‖‖‖‖‖‖‖‖‖

I remember Mama, and the love that she gave.
Kneeling by her bedside, I can still hear Mama say,
"The people are depending on you, Shirley,
don't you let them down."
I remember Mama in a happy way.
We went to school with holes in our shoes.
We didn't have much, but the Lord saw us through.
Mama kept the family together.
I remember Mama in a happy way.
She packed our lunch in an old, greasy bag.
It might have seemed empty, but it was more than others had.
It had a lot of love way down deep inside.
And I remember Mama in a happy way.
Now Mama is sleeping in the bosom of Jesus Christ.
Somehow I know she's smiling on us right now.
One day I'll see her again, how happy I will be.
And I remember Mama in a happy way.
My brothers and sisters, they're living far apart.

Although my mama's gone, she's right here in our hearts.
We're all going to pull together and stay in the holy way.
I remember Mama in a happy way.
—"I Remember Mama"

AND THE WORD

She watches over the ways of her household,
And does not eat the bread of idleness.
Her children rise up and call her blessed;
Her husband also, and he praises her:
"Many daughters have done well,
But you excel them all."
Charm is deceitful and beauty is passing,
But a woman who fears the LORD, she shall be praised.
—Proverbs 31:27–30

———— I can still see my mother in the kitchen today, alternately sitting in a chair and leaning on her walker, while preparing dinner for her family. Or I see her sitting in her room at the midnight hour waiting for me to return home from a weekend singing engagement. I can still hear the kind, sweet sound of her voice as she asks, "Shirley Ann, is that you?" as I come through the door. I yet smell the fresh, clean scent of her hair, and I will forever feel the gentle touch of her hands. Even though her hands were toughened by work, they always felt like the softest hands in the world when she touched me. When she prepared meals for the people she loved she always wore her favorite apron. It was old and worn from the many meals that she prepared wearing it, but she could never bring herself to throw it away. She had the prettiest chocolate-brown eyes, which always sparkled with love from behind the wire-rimmed glasses that she wore. If I saw her like that once, I saw her like that thousands of times. She is my mama, and she has a special place in any story of my life.

I loved Mama more than anyone else in the world. She meant the world to me. No one had any greater influence on my life than she did. There was absolutely no one that I loved, admired, and respected more than Mama. All of my brothers and sisters felt the same way about her as I did. And in Mama's eyes, we were all special. Whatever we may have lacked materially, Mama more than made up for it with her love. She imparted to us a keen sense of being loved and of belonging. Although I knew she loved us equally, I always felt my relationship with her was very special. But, of course, all the children felt they had a particularly special relationship with Mama. My love for her was deeper than words could express. Our relationship was extremely close. Perhaps I clung to her closely because my father died when I was so young. Mama taught me about life. She instilled in me, through precept and example, the meaning of love and the importance of giving and sharing. Mama devoted herself to her family. She worked hard and made endless sacrifices to raise her children, grandchildren, and even great-grandchildren. She gave us a sense of unity. A lady of quiet dignity, she taught us to hold our heads up high and appreciate who God had made us. Without a question, Mama epitomized what the Lord had in mind when He created mothers.

When I speak with so much love about my mother, people sometimes think she never had any problems with me. When I became an adult she never did, but as a child I was often disobedient and sometimes talked back to her. When I did, she responded accordingly. She believed that if you spared the rod, you spoiled the child. Believe me, none of us were spoiled children. Despite her handicap, she was capable of reprimanding her children when necessary.

The second worst whipping I received from Mama (the Popsicle episode being the worst) happened when I was about eleven years old. Mama had told my sister Anne and me to bring in the clothes off the line in the backyard because it looked as if it was going to rain. Anne and I didn't want to bring in the clothes. I stepped to the door, looked up at the sky, saw it blue and clear, and told Mama, "There isn't a cloud anywhere. The clothes don't need to be brought in."

Mama didn't argue; she just repeated her instructions. "I know it's going to rain, so bring the clothes in off the line." With that, she turned and walked out of the room.

Instead of bringing in the clothes, Anne and I went to the park to play.

All that week, we were repeatedly disobedient to Mama. She kept telling us, "I'm putting it on the shelf." That was her way of telling us that we were trying her patience and that she wouldn't forget our defiance.

By the end of the week, Mama's fictional shelf had gotten very full. She told my brother Solomon to go outside and bring in a good switch. We knew what that meant. Solomon climbed up in an old apple tree in the backyard and broke off a tree limb and brought it in the house, but Mama didn't use it right then. Anne and I misread this nonaction by Mama and went to bed that night with a false sense of security. We didn't realize that Mama had her master plan set. In the stillness of the night I felt a cold draft on my legs. I pulled at the covers and said, "Anne, give me some cover."

Anne said, "I don't have the cover."

Then I felt a hand. "Anne," I whispered. "Is that your hand?"

Anne said, "Here's my hand."

About that time, Mama said, "Get up, and come to me like you came into the world." I knew I didn't have on any clothes when I came into the world.

We had on red flannel pajamas, with ten buttons down the front and two buttons in the back. Mama said, "Unbutton all twelve of those buttons."

We knew we were in trouble. Anne jumped up and ran under the bed. I tried to squeeze between a rollaway cot that was standing by our bed.

Mama did not move from her seat. With a firm voice she said, "I'm not going to move, and if you run, you better keep running and don't come back. I've told you all week to do your chores, but all you did was talk back and didn't listen to me at all. You've been disobedient, hardheaded, and rebellious, and I am sick and tired of it. If you live in this house, you will obey me. Now which one of you is going first?"

We knew we didn't have any choice but to take our medicine, regardless of how unpleasant. When it was over, Mama didn't have any more problems with Anne or me doing our chores. We didn't want another whipping like that.

Mama never ignored our disobedient actions. We called her the caseworker, because if she got on your case, she would work you over. She always contended that she would rather discipline us than have the police beat us.

Many people today don't believe in disciplining a child in that manner, but it worked for us. I believe we wouldn't have as many problems with our youth if parents, teachers, churches, and neighbors interacted to develop and nurture our children. Contrary to popular belief, it does take a whole village to raise a child.

Thank God, I didn't receive many whippings from Mama, but when I did they had a lasting impression on me. It was

Mama's way of reminding me that there was a wrong way of doing things and then there was Mama's way. And of course, Mama's way was always the right way. I never doubted Mama's love. Even when she chastised us, she did it in love. She loved her children more than she loved anything else in the world. It was her desire that we grow up to be good, productive citizens.

Later, when I began singing in churches, Mama admonished me about the importance of living the life I was singing about. She would always say, "Shirley Ann, the people are depending on you. If you mess up, not only are you failing yourself, but you are failing others, and most importantly, you are failing God." She told me that my life had become a public statement for Jesus and that people would rather see a sermon than hear a sermon. If I was going to preach and sing about Jesus, it was my responsibility to make sure my life exemplified whom I was representing. Mama imbedded that principle in me from the onset of my ministry, and it remains in me today. I want my life to draw others to Christ and not repel them. I also want to be a beacon and not a stumbling block to others. The Lord had blessed me with a tremendous gift, and with it came a tremendous responsibility. The Bible lets us know that "to whom much is given, from him much will be required."

My mother personified the kind of life I should live. She was my example and my guide. Mama taught me to love everyone regardless of race, educational level, or social standing. She treated everyone with respect and kindness. Whatever she had she willingly shared with others. Everyone in our community was in some way the recipient of Mama's hospitality, even our insurance agents.

In those days, insurance agents made house calls to collect premiums paid for insurance coverage. The agents would come by our house with their little black books to collect the fifty cents a month that Mama paid for the insurance policies she carried for herself and the children. After they would record the payments and put their books back in their pockets. You would expect them to take their money and proceed to the next customer's house, but that seldom happened. Most of the time they ended up having dinner with us, because Mama would always invite them to eat before they left, and they rarely refused.

They would sit right at the table with us, unloose their shirt collars, and lean forward to eat. Boy, did they eat! These insurance agents would leave with their stomachs full of Mama's pinto beans, collard greens, potato salad, and fried chicken. Sometimes I would tease Mama, telling her that the only reason they ate was because they thought they wouldn't get paid next time if they didn't.

Mama provided everyone with that kind of attention. The children in our neighborhood especially loved her. They came over often, not just to play with me or my brothers and sisters, but to see Mama and enjoy some of her good cooking.

Every preacher who crossed the threshold of our door was treated to Mama's hospitality and fed a delicious meal. I particularly feel that one of the reasons Mama was so blessed is because she never neglected to feed God's messengers. Just think, if God promises to give you a prophet's reward for giving a drink of water, can you imagine your blessing for providing a whole meal!

Given our financial circumstances, Mama's meals weren't too elaborate. But that didn't matter. If I heard her once, I heard her a thousand times say, "Such as I have . . ." Such as she had, she willingly gave to any and all who came her way.

After my father died, we lived on a fixed income, most of it from the government. Even then, Mama found a way to subsidize our income by selling merchandise from the back porch of our house. I guess you can say that we had somewhat of a family store right on our porch. The vendors came to our house just as they would to a corner grocery store and sold Mama wholesale merchandise. She, in turn, added a small markup to the price and sold it for a marginal profit.

I don't know if she needed a permit in those days, but no one ever said anything to her about it. She sold bubble gum, candy, sodas, and a few other odds and ends from the Caesar Store on the Porch!

When I think of Mama, I remember all the valuable lessons she imparted to me. No, she didn't sit me down and say, "Here are ten keys to living a successful life." But she did teach me those keys by precept and example.

One thing Mama taught me was humility. She always emphasized that regardless of who we were or what we achieved, we should remember that the Lord gave it to us and it was not because of any goodness of our own but only by His grace.

When I told her I had won my first Grammy (a story I'll relate later), we were sitting at the kitchen table at our home in Durham. She listened quietly as I explained what the Grammy was and what it might mean to my career. I was going on and on, and it was obvious that I was elated over this accomplishment.

When I finished, she reached over the table and put her hands on mine. With a soft voice and a gentle smile, she said, "I'm so proud of you, Shirley Ann. The Lord is blessing you. Stay grateful, stay humble, and never take God's goodness for granted. Never forget those who helped you get where you are. And always remember the Lord made it all possible." To this day, whenever I win an award or receive any recognition, Mama's words play back in my mind, and my response is always, "To God be the glory."

Mama also demonstrated to me the necessity of working hard. I saw her working day after day and year after year washing clothes, cooking food, combing hair, and making beds. She did the work of four people and somehow managed to do it all even with her handicap.

She always said, "Don't sit back and wait for someone else. Some things will get done only if you do them yourself."

I've found that to be true, and I have lived by this philosophy, "Lord, if you will just crack the door, I will kick it down for your glory!" In other words, if the Lord shows me what to do, I don't hesitate in trying to get it done.

My mother instructed me that you need "grit, grace, gut, God, and gumption" to make it in life. Take the gifts the Lord has given you, roll up your sleeves, and go to work.

I've always felt protective of my mother. As a child, I occasionally got into confrontations with other children who maliciously made fun of her and called her names because of her crippled leg. One boy in particular seemed to take pleasure in making cruel remarks about her. One day he made the mistake of calling her "Old Crooked Leg." A couple of my brothers and sisters and I caught him out by himself and gave him a few hard "love taps," convincing him that he should never say anything unkind about our mother again.

Mama found out about that fight. She didn't spank me, but instead sat me down to talk about it. She said, "Shirley Ann, fighting doesn't solve anything. I want you to stop this fighting."

I shook my head. "But he said a bad thing about you, Mama."

"He doesn't know me," she said. "So what he says about me doesn't matter."

"But I'm not going to let him say those bad things about you."

"Yes, you are. It doesn't matter what he or anyone else says. They're just trying to build themselves up by tearing somebody else down. Let it go, Shirley Ann. Let it go."

I nodded my head, indicating I agreed with her, but I didn't. This time I didn't follow her advice. Whenever anyone said anything cruel about my mother, they automatically had a fight on their hands.

Not only was I protective of my mother, but I always wanted to provide for her and help make ends meet around the house. Whenever I received an offering from singing in churches I brought every penny home and put the money in Mama's hand, telling her, "This is what the people in Greensboro (or Winston-Salem or wherever I sang) sent to you this week, Mama." Many times it was just a small amount, but she would always smile at me and give thanks to the Lord. Her smile of approval meant more to me than anything else in the world.

When the Lord really began to bless my career and I had the opportunity to go on the road professionally, I hesitated because I didn't want to leave Mama. As much as I wanted to go, I would have given it all up if she had said to stay. Thankfully, she knew this was the Lord's will for me, and she encouraged me to go.

Mama always supported us in what we wanted to do as long as she thought the Lord was in it. She didn't try to hold us back or try to make us do things her way. If she could see the Lord's hand in what we were doing, she gave us her blessing.

Mama's love is the inspiration for many of my songs. In

songs such as "No Charge," "Don't Drive Your Mama Away," "Faded Rose," and "I Love You, Mama," I try to remind people of the blessing of having a good mother and how they should cherish her while she is yet alive. My song "I Remember Mama" ministers to anyone whose mother has gone on to be with the Lord and who struggle with the grief caused by her passing. I try to deal with those feelings in song and simultaneously inspire them to hold on to and cherish those wonderful memories.

"Don't Drive Your Mama Away" tells the story of a mother who has two sons. One son succeeds and becomes a doctor. The other is unsuccessful, stays in trouble, struggles, has no job, makes no money, and finally moves away from home.

As the years pass, the mother gets old and moves in with the son who is an accomplished physician. But as the mother ages, the son's wife convinces him that they should put her in a nursing home. The son tries to ease his conscience by telling his mother that she will have nothing but the best there. But when the wayward son meets them as they are en route to the nursing home, he stops them. After finding out where they are going, he says to his mother, "I'm not riding in a limousine, neither do I live in a fine house, but you're my mother, and I am your son, and if you want to you can come home with me."

This kind of song teaches a lesson people need to hear, a lesson of caring, sharing, and demonstrating love for the one who loved and cared for you unconditionally. Everywhere I travel I tell young people, "Don't allow your mother to want for anything; don't spend her money needlessly talking long distance on the phone; don't work all week and then not give her anything to help out. Your mother and father are your best friends." I encourage people to care for their parents while they have them, because sooner than any of us expect, death takes them away from us.

Over the years since the age of twelve, I tried to take care of my mother. After my career began to render some financial gain, one of the first things I did was to buy her a house.

I managed to do this after eight years on the road as a full-time gospel singer traveling with the Caravans (a time I'll describe in the next chapter). I had saved about five thousand dollars from my earnings and had decided to move back home to Durham from Chicago where I lived at the time.

Mama had sent my sister Anne and a friend of ours, Norma Jean Burton, to Chicago to help me bring back my few belongings. With their help, I loaded up everything I owned—a little bed, a few pots and pans, a television, some silverware, and a mattress.

With those possessions in a U-Haul rental truck behind my car, we drove south and came into Durham from Interstate 85. On the way home, we turned right at the downtown Durham exit and proceeded up Roxboro Street, which then turned into Mangum Street. We had gone through one stop light, and as we approached the second one, the Spirit of the Lord spoke to me and said to turn right. I turned right, which was in the opposite direction from our house.

Anne turned and looked at me, with a funny look on her face.

"Where are you going, Shirley Ann?" she asked. "We don't live this way."

"I don't know," I said. "But I felt impressed of the Lord to turn onto this street."

"You're crazy girl," she said. "Let's go on home. I'm tired, and you're getting us lost."

Driving slowly down that street, I suddenly knew why I had turned in the opposite direction. At that moment, the Lord spoke to my spirit and told me He had a house for Mama in that block.

With mounting excitement, I scanned the houses. Which one, which one? Then I saw it—an empty, white Victorian-style house, a small white porch on the front, sitting in the middle of the block. A big house, at least ten rooms, I guessed. Instantly, I knew the Lord had chosen this house for my mother.

In a hurry, I turned into the driveway, parked, and jumped out of the car. Anne and Norma Jean followed me, telling me the whole time I needed to get back in the car and get away from that house. "You're crazy, Shirley," Anne repeated. "You're crazy, and you're going to get us arrested."

I paid no attention. "God told me to do this," I said, not looking back. Intuitively knowing the front door would be locked, I walked around to the back and onto the porch. Standing on a box, I reached up, feeling for a key on the ledge over the door. Sure enough, I found one.

With Anne still telling me to stop, I unlocked the door and walked inside. From the minute I saw that house, I loved it. It did have ten rooms, including three bathrooms, and a dining room. I was sold.

I turned to Anne and Norma Jean. "Let's get my stuff," I said.

Their mouths dropped open.

"You're not moving your stuff in here," said Anne, "You'll get arrested for sure."

"Let's get my stuff," I said. "This is our house."

I walked past them to the car to get my belongings. This was going to be Mama's house, so I might as well claim it. At that point, Anne and Norma Jean reluctantly gave up. With their help, I brought in my things, hung sheets over the windows so people couldn't see inside, and settled down for the night.

With Anne still telling me I was crazy, I slept in that house that very night. The next morning, I woke up, found out who owned the place, put down five thousand dollars on it, and told Mama to get ready to move. She did, and I never slept in the house on Simmons Street again. With Mama and my sisters and their children, I moved into the house. We remodeled it, put new siding on, lowered the ceilings, put in a new furnace, and furnished it just like Mama wanted. Within two years I paid off the mortgage of that house the Lord had led me to for Mama, and she lived there until her demise.

I'll never forget the feeling of happiness I felt the first time some of Mama's relatives visited her in her new place. She was so excited about her new home that she asked us to show them around the house. She happily expressed to them, "I've got my own bathroom with a bathtub, and the water is always hot." She loved her new house, and I loved having the opportunity to give back to her for all she had given to me.

I'll never forget the last Christmas we shared with Mama. In many ways it was typical of all the rest. Her whole family—children, brothers, sisters, nieces, nephews, grandchildren, great-grandchildren—all gathered on Christmas Day at Mama's house. We all crowded into the living room around the tree. The tree, covered with shiny lights, was placed in just the right spot so Mama could see it from her bedroom when she went to bed every night.

As usual Mama, the nucleus of the family, took her place in her special chair, while the other family members positioned themselves all around the living room.

We began as we did every year. We first sang Christmas carols, and then we moved around the family circle with everybody offering testimony or praise to the Lord. We reminisced about the good and related how the Lord had brought us through the difficult times of the year. We thanked Him for grace and mercy. Mama had always taught us, "In everything give thanks; for this is the will of God in Christ Jesus for you." This time of the year always gave us a time to reflect: Had we done all we could to please the Lord over the last year? Had we walked as closely to the Lord as we should have?

I believe one of the reasons Mama instituted this family tradition was to make us review our spiritual lives, kind of like an annual checkup. From time to time, Christmas became an opportunity for me to rededicate myself to the Lord.

As a child, those devotional services had seemed to take forever. I always wanted to hurry up and open my presents. But that last year we had Mama with us, I wanted it to last forever. Somehow, even then, I sensed she might not make many more Christmas gatherings. I didn't want to think about it, but I knew it was inevitable.

Mama had suffered a stroke in the summer and had grown weaker by the day. I wanted our family devotion on Christmas to go on and on, never to end. But it did. Everybody in the room had their turn, spoke their praise, or said their Scripture. Now, it was time for the prayer. Always before, Mama had offered the prayer.

I'll never forget those prayers. Supplications to the Lord for the health and happiness of all her children and later her grandchildren. I grew up listening to Mama pray, and I don't think any child could ever hear sweeter words than the words I heard my mother pray.

That last year, as always, we turned to Mama to pray. The room fell quiet. Even the little children seemed to lean in closer to listen. Mama tried to speak. Nothing much came out, but she kept trying. We all leaned in closer. I stood up and bent over to listen. I heard what she was mumbling.

"I'll be all right after a while," she said. "I'll be all right after a while."

Those words still ring in my heart, even to this day. *I'll be all right after a while.* Looking back now, I know what she meant. She would soon pass from this world into the presence of the Lord. But at the time I didn't know that. I thought she meant she would get well soon, that she would recover. But, of course, she didn't.

We had her with us for almost another eleven months. On November 8, 1986, at the age of eighty-four, Mama fell asleep in Jesus. We all struggled to get through that Christmas. We kept all the traditions she had taught us, including our testimonies and our Christmas carols, but we couldn't help but cry all through the ceremony.

When I first began my career as a singer, Mama gave me some advice I never forgot: "Don't let God down. Don't let the people down. And don't let me down." In a sense, she gave me my gospel commission with those words.

Even though the Lord has blessed me far beyond what even Mama imagined, her words have kept me rooted and grounded and committed to the cause of the gospel. My mother's words have also kept me aware of my responsibilities as an ambassador of the Lord Jesus Christ.

Though she has been with the Lord for eleven years, I yet mourn her passing. I miss her smile and her warm touch. Often, when I sing, I find myself watching the older mothers in the audience, and I sing to them. It is no wonder that I find myself clinging to the older mothers in my church.

At the same time that I grieve the loss of Mama, I also rejoice that I'll see her again. I believe that with all my heart. And so I give thanks to the Lord for all the special times that we shared, and I look forward to an eternity with her and my father and the Lord who loves and made us all.

CHAPTER FIVE
On the Road with the Caravans

Have you ever walked the floor, all night long
wondering how you were going to pay your bills,
then a still small voice said,
"Be strong, sometimes struggle is My will.
I'm never late, I'm always on time,
get ready for your miracle, move to the front of the line."

Today is your day, today is your day
Get ready, get ready, get ready.
You're next in line for a miracle.
—"You're Next in Line for a Miracle"

AND THE WORD

Trust in the LORD with all your heart,
And lean not on your own understanding;
In all your ways acknowledge Him,
And He shall direct your paths.
—Proverbs 3:5–6

THE stories of the way people get their big breaks in life always fascinate me. The model who gets discovered while serving tables in a restaurant, the actor who is found while working out in a gym with a movie agent, or the athlete who gets discovered while playing street ball with friends. Although their dreams seemed impossible, somehow they became a reality. Even though they may have worked long and hard hours preparing themselves for their desired vocation, almost every person who achieves a certain level of success in life can point back to some event that opened the door for them.

In many aspects my story is just as dramatic, in that it illustrates the precision of God's timing. I had been singing for a number of years and was well known throughout some of the southern states, but nothing beyond the circle of churches where I ministered in song. My career had reached a certain level and didn't seem to be progressing. But when you walk in God's will, everything flows according to His plan and His timetable for your life.

In August 1958 I found myself at a crossroads in my life. I had completed my freshman year at North Carolina College, and it was almost time to register for the fall session. I knew my mother didn't have the money to pay for my tuition or buy my books, and beyond that I knew that, given our financial situation, the chance of my completing college was almost nonexistent. And to be honest, I really didn't know if going to college was what I wanted to do. However, I was sure that I wanted to sing. As far back as I can remember I have always loved to sing. Singing for the Lord was in my heart and in my soul. It was my heritage. I sang all the time, and I knew I wanted to sing for the rest of my life.

During this transition period, I attended a concert in Raleigh, North Carolina, at the Memorial Auditorium. The Caravans, one of the best-known black female gospel groups, was featured along with several other gospel artists, including the Soul Stirrers, the Blind Boys, the Nightingales, and the Original Gospel Harmonettes.

I sat in the auditorium, enjoying the concert, clapping and singing along with the rest of the audience. It was a hot summer day, and the air-conditioning appeared not to be working. But I was so engrossed in the performances that I was unaware of the stifling heat.

When the Caravans came onstage to sing, I noticed they had only three singers—Albertina Walker, Inez Andrews, and Sarah McKissick. Eddie Williams played the piano.

I thought within myself, Wow, how will they achieve a perfect three-part harmony with a lead and only two background singers? They needed a fourth part, and I was confident that I was the person for the job. Even as a young girl I was always self-assured.

For a few minutes I sat there, trying to think how to let them know that I could sing that part without sounding too conceited. After all, how does a little girl from Durham approach the best-known female gospel group of all time and tell them she should be singing with them?

I knew, however, I couldn't let this opportunity pass. It

was now or never. I kept thinking, If Albertina Walker, the leader of the Caravans, could only hear me sing, I could convince her I had what it took to be a Caravan singer.

When an intermission occurred, I found Dorothy Love Coates, the lead singer of the Gospel Harmonettes, and said, "Will you tell that lady I can sing the fourth part she's missing in her group?"

To my surprise, Dorothy did just that, even though I didn't think that she would. She later told me that she mentioned to Albertina that there was a little girl out in the audience who said she could sing the missing part in the group's background.

Albertina just shrugged it off, not paying any attention to the suggestion. I'm sure I wasn't the only would-be singer who had tried to avail herself of the opportunity to try to sing with them.

The concert ended late that afternoon, and my efforts to become a member of the Caravans had failed. But I didn't give up. I saw a second chance, and I've always been one to work hard to make the most of my chances.

That same night, all of the same groups were scheduled to sing in Kinston, North Carolina, a small city not far from Raleigh. I caught a ride to the concert, and when the doors opened I walked in and took a seat near the front. I was determined to make this second chance work.

During the concert I took out a piece of paper and wrote a request that said, *Please call on Shirley Caesar to sing a solo.* I gave the request to an usher to take to the stage.

With my heart pounding, I watched the usher carry it to the mistress of ceremonies. After reading it, she moved to a microphone and sarcastically announced, "We have a request that someone wants to hear Shirley Caesar sing a solo. Is Shirley Caesar here?"

I almost hit the ceiling when I jumped out of my seat. "Here I am," I shouted. "Over here."

I hit the stage running; my legs were weak and shaking from both nerves and happiness. All I had ever wanted to do had come down to this moment. If I could sing well, I might be on my way, not to fame and fortune, but to the full use of the gifts that I knew the Lord had given me.

I told the mistress of ceremonies I wanted to sing Thomas A. Dorsey's song, "The Lord Will Make a Way Somehow."

Like a ship that's tossed and driven,
battered by the angry sea.
When the storms of life are raging,
and the fury falls on me.
Lord, I wonder what I've done,
to make this race so hard to run.
But I said to my soul, "Take courage,
the Lord will make a way somehow."

Through that song I voiced the sentiments of my heart. The Lord will make a way somehow! Proverbs 3:6 says, "In all your ways acknowledge Him, / and He shall direct your paths." If we live by faith and entrust ourselves to the Lord's care, He will lead us in the ways we should go. I believed that then, and I believe it now.

I poured my heart and soul into the song, and I could tell from the audience's response that they believed what I was singing. Obviously the Lord had proven to many of them that He would in fact make a way somehow! The Holy Spirit was definitely in the house. I heard Albertina speaking behind me. She said, "I want that little girl." I had never heard sweeter words. They set off a chain of events that would influence the rest of my life. My professional career in gospel music began with those words. The Lord was giving me a larger platform from which I could share Him with the world.

After the concert, I stood around talking to people, still amazed at what the Lord had just done. I felt a hand on my shoulder and turned around. Behind me stood Albertina. She had a smile on her face. She asked, "Can you travel?"

I know she didn't think I was old enough. When she looked at me, instead of seeing the young lady that I really was, she saw a tiny little girl wearing bobby socks who appeared much younger.

I paused for a couple of seconds, not because I didn't want to go but because I knew it would mean a whole new life for me. I didn't want to jump into things too fast. Also, I knew I had to do one primary thing before I could answer. It was the most important thing of all. I had to ask Mama. I said to her, "I don't know. I have to ask my mother."

Albertina said, "I understand. Go home and talk it over with your mother, and someone will be in touch with you next week."

I went home that night and excitedly told Mama everything that had happened. I knew going on the road with the Caravans would mean that finishing college was out of the question. It would mean leaving home and moving to Chicago. But above all, it would mean having to leave Mama. After all, I had only traveled between North and South Carolina, Virginia, and Washington, D.C., and the world outside of those narrow confines seemed mysterious and frightening. Mama knew this was definitely a crossroad in my life, and she did not want to stand in the way of my possible chance-of-a-lifetime opportunity. And although she knew there wasn't any money to send me back to school, before she answered she said, "Let's pray about it."

Mama and I prayed about what I should do. Though I

wasn't with her all night, I believe Mama prayed most of the night. I stayed up a long time also, thinking and hoping and praying.

The next day, Reverend C. L. Franklin, Aretha Franklin's father, called my mother. He often preached in places where Albertina and the Caravans sang, and they were good friends.

Albertina had asked him to call my mother to reassure her that I would be taken care of if she would allow me to join the Caravans. By then I knew I wanted to go. With great joy and excitement, I said to Mama, "Please say yes, I can go. Please tell him I can go, tell him I can go."

Mama nodded her head. "Shirley is of age. She can go if this is what she wants."

To my surprise, hearing Mama's consent suddenly gave me a spell of cold feet. It hit me like a ton of bricks! Traveling with the Caravans meant I really would have to be away from my family. So there I was with mixed emotions. I wanted to go, I wanted to be a Caravan, but yet I didn't want to leave my mom! But with reservations, Mama assured me that I should go. After praying she now felt that this was God's will for my life. She said to me, "All you have ever wanted to do is to sing for the Lord. Go with my blessings."

The next day, I sold my biology book, which had cost thirty-two dollars, for only eight dollars, and used the money to buy a bus ticket from Durham to Washington, D.C., where I was to meet the Caravans. With that ticket in hand, I kissed my family good-bye, climbed on the bus with just a few clothes, and headed north. That evening, upon arrival, I checked into the Casbah Hotel. This was the first time I had ever stayed in a hotel. The Caravans were supposed to meet me there, but they hadn't arrived.

That hotel was the pits! It looked like a hotel for transients. Paint was peeling off the walls, and the carpet was dirty and stained. I didn't feel safe there, and it wasn't much of a welcome for a young girl away from home by herself for the first time. I felt so alone. I wanted someone with me, and no one was there to meet me. But that wasn't the worst of it. Within a few hours, I found out just how different this new world was from the one I left behind.

I went downstairs to get something to eat, and, too fearful to do anything else, I went immediately back to my room. With great fear in my heart, I locked my door with the chain and dead bolt. I went to bed early that night, hoping and praying that by morning Albertina and the other group members would be there.

Within an hour or so, I heard a knock on my door. I couldn't imagine who it might be. A man's voice followed the sound of the knock. I recognized the voice of a man I had met earlier downstairs in the hotel lobby. He was a member of another singing group also staying in the hotel. They were featured artists for the same concert at which the Caravans were to perform on the following night.

Since I had seen his group perform on stage many times, I thought it would be safe to see what he wanted. While keeping the chain attached, I unlocked the door and looked out. The man stood there with a silly grin on his face.

I said, "Yes, what do you want?"

"I was wondering if I could come in and get you to bless my cross for me?" he said. He held out this huge cross he was wearing around his neck.

Even though I was a young, innocent girl from a small town in North Carolina, I wasn't stupid. I wasn't about to fall for that kind of line.

I slammed the door and shouted through the wall, "I'll do it tomorrow." And that was the end of that.

Years later, that same man, whom I am very fond of today,

has come to know the Lord in the pardon of his sins. He has repeatedly apologized for his actions that night. He told me there were so many things in his past that he regretted. And one of them was that he had used that same line to lure and seduce so many young women. He said, "A lot of women fell for that line I tried to use on you."

"But it didn't work with me," I reminded him.

"No, it didn't," he agreed. "You were ready for guys like me." Then he smiled.

With the armor of God and the protective covering of my mother's prayers, I survived attacks like that on the road.

The only good thing about that night was that it began to establish the fact among the groups on the road that I was serious about my commitment to Christ.

It wasn't long after that incident that many of the groups on the road gave me a pet name. They started calling me "The Bishop." At the time I didn't understand the essence of the name, but I soon realized what they were trying to say. This was simply their way of showing their respect for me.

The Caravans arrived from Chicago the next day, and I joined them. We rehearsed that afternoon, and I performed on stage with them that night. My career as a Caravan had begun.

Because Inez Andrews was away in Birmingham, Alabama, attending a family member's funeral service, Albertina asked me if I could sing any of her songs. I replied, "Yes, and I can sing some of your songs too!"

Albertina didn't respond. I guess this wasn't the first time she had met spirited young singers. My first songs were "I'm Willing to Wait" and "He'll Wash You Whiter than Snow."

When Inez returned, I continued to co-lead some of her songs with her. And at times, we all interchangeably sang each other's songs. However, for the most part, we tried to find the songs that would enhance our voice quality and become characteristic of each of us. When you think of the song "Mary, Don't You Weep," you automatically think of Inez Andrews. When you think of "Sweeping Through the City," you think of Shirley Caesar. And when you think of "Lord, Keep Me Day by Day," you think of Albertina Walker. It didn't matter that I didn't have any songs of my own; I was just elated to be traveling from city to city, state to state, singing and sharing the gospel of Jesus Christ in song. Regardless of what song I sang, I poured my heart and soul into it.

I was enthusiastic about everything I did. The first time I sang with the Caravans at the Apollo Theater in New York, I was so excited I ran upstairs to the top floor in about thirty seconds, taking those stairs three at a time. I had so much energy I didn't know what to do with it all. Over the years I guess it would be safe to say I used up a great deal of it in the process of just learning about life, because I was very naive in those days.

I remember going to Kentucky for the first time. Several members of the group spoke of it as the Bluegrass State. I said, "Wonderful, I'm going to get a chance to see some blue grass." I thought it would look like the sky or a robin's egg. When we crossed the state line, I kept looking for the blue grass. I remember riding across the whole state, staring out the window, and never once seeing grass that even remotely looked blue!

I spent eight years with the Caravans and in the interim picked up a number of other nicknames. Some people started calling me the "Fireball." A few named me "Human Dynamo," while others called me "House Wrecker," because they said I brought the house down. I appreciated all the superlatives, but I knew it was not I, but Christ who lived in me, and that it is the anointing that destroys the yoke. So whatever positive changes were happening in people's lives because of our ministry on stage, I always said, "To God be the glory."

The one nickname I especially appreciated was the one Albertina called me, and that was "Little Trouper." She called me this because I always projected so much energy into our performances, and she said regardless of how bad I felt I always made sure that I never missed a scheduled Caravan performance.

For the entire time I sang with the Caravans, I never missed a concert. I never got too sick or too hoarse to sing, although many times I was extremely tired and my voice was raspy and dry. Even when I came down with the flu or bronchitis, which I did every now and again, the Lord always blessed me with the perseverance and the stamina to press on. Once every last member of the group caught the flu, even the musicians. Everybody had chills and fever and was coughing like they were about to die. For two weeks while everyone recuperated at home, I fulfilled all of our scheduled concert engagements. To say the least I was nervous, not because I didn't think I could do it, but I didn't want to jeopardize in any way the performance excellence the Caravans were known for. When I stepped out on stage for the first time without them, I looked out over the people in that vast audience. Their faces were turned expectantly toward me, and a wave of doubt swept over me. The Caravans were the number one gospel group, and I was the new girl in the group. No one really knew me. Would this audience receive me? Would they be disappointed that the entire group was not present? Could I fill the shoes of all the others?

Before I went onstage, I said a prayer, asking the Lord to take control of the service, to use me for His glory, and let His presence be felt throughout the auditorium. Then, taking a deep breath, I went out.

When I began singing, it seemed that the audience was a little quiet. The more I sang, the more I began to feel the presence of the Holy Spirit, and I could sense that the audience was also warming up. Eventually it appeared that everyone there was praising the Lord. I could hear shouts of "Praise God," "Hallelujah," and "Thank You, Jesus" reverberating throughout the room. People were standing and waving their hands in gestures of worship. Surely, the Lord was in the building! With the Blind Boys of Alabama behind me, I completed the concert. As we left the stage, the power of God was yet moving among the people, touching, saving, healing, and doing a new thing in their lives. I thought to myself, Who wouldn't serve a God like this?

For the next two weeks, with the Blind Boys or the Soul Stirrers as my backup, I represented the Caravans in churches and auditoriums where we were scheduled to perform. After each concert, I turned over all the earnings to Albertina, who in turn paid every member of our group. That's the way it was; we were all paid whether we could sing or not.

Although I've always persevered to make every scheduled performance, there was once I thought I would definitely miss a concert or two. I was so sick that I just didn't think I would be able to sing. The one thing that kept me going was my commitment to the Caravans; I knew Albertina was depending upon me. After all, I was her little trouper.

We were en route to Birmingham, Alabama, from a Saturday night concert and had at least two hundred miles more to travel. We were hungry and began looking for a restaurant to get something to eat. Eddie Williams, our musician, was driving and noticed a lot of young people standing outside of a restaurant.

Eddie said to Albertina, "We're coming up on a place to eat. I don't think we are going to find anywhere else between here and Birmingham. Let's stop here." As it turned out, this restaurant was an all-night juke joint. We pulled up and parked, and all of us went in. There was a lot of loud blasting music, swearing, and cigarette smoke. We ordered our food to go because we wanted to get out of there and time was of the essence. We were scheduled to sing on the radio that Sunday morning at 7:30. It was customary in those days for gospel groups to do live radio performances in an effort to promote the concerts. I remember ordering a sliced-pork sandwich. Once our order arrived, we got back in the car and drove away.

As we headed toward Birmingham that night and began eating our food, something happened to me I will never forget. A few miles down the road I began having severe abdominal cramps. I doubled over in pain from obvious food poisoning. I was extremely nauseated, so I asked Eddie to pull over to the side of the road to let me out of the car. For about five minutes I was upchucking. That helped for a little while, but then the cramps began again. For several hours, it went like that. Pull over, get sick, drive a few miles, pull over, and get sick. Unfortunately, this put us behind schedule.

All I could think of was that if we kept stopping for me, we wouldn't make it to the radio station on time. They decided not to stop again, but I was still sick. I did the only thing I could do. I rolled down the car window and let it fly. I left my sickness all over the asphalt on that Alabama road.

After arriving in Birmingham around 6:00 A.M., we checked into the hotel. I rushed to my room, fell on the bed, and curled up in pain. A few minutes later one of the group members knocked on the door and said, "Hurry and get dressed. We've got to go straight to the radio station."

I shouted out, "I can't go. I'm in too much pain."

About five minutes later Albertina came to my room and said, "I need you at the radio station this morning."

I replied, "I'm just too sick."

When she left, I found myself getting dressed to go with them. And I did.

Even though I was not at my best, I was yet able to sing a strong alto behind Inez Andrews on "Mary, Don't You Weep" and then follow it up with "Hallelujah, 'Tis Done."

I can only say that God gave me the strength and the stamina to carry on even while physically impaired.

Those years with the Caravans weren't always easy ones. The schedules we kept and the conditions under which we traveled were very trying. We would pack our bags and all six of us would pile into our Cadillac, sometimes traveling all day to get to a concert that night. Once we arrived, we only had time to get a bite to eat, get dressed, and go onstage. Often we sang in churches. At other times we sang in auditoriums. Occasionally we had the privilege to sing in large places like Radio City Music Hall and Madison Square Garden, but most places we performed were certainly smaller than the huge stadiums or arenas where many gospel artists perform today.

The gospel music industry wasn't nearly as organized as it is today. We didn't have booking agents or legal advisers. The level of professionalism then was not what it is today.

We did almost everything on our own. When we got a call from someone, we checked the calendar to see if we were available, made reservations at some local hotel in the concert city, and packed up and headed out.

Sometimes, we would sing for two or three hours and then receive twenty-five to fifty dollars each for our work. Racial discrimination kept us out of the more decent hotels and restaurants, but even if it hadn't, it wouldn't have mattered. We didn't have the money to stay in the nicer places anyway.

When we weren't on the road, I stayed at Albertina's house. I slept on her couch and paid her two dollars a night. At the time I didn't think I should have had to pay the money, but after Albertina sat me down and explained it to me, I understood.

"I don't need the two dollars," she said. "I'm simply trying to teach you responsibility."

Looking back, I understand what she was doing. She was showing me that regardless of where I go or what I do, nothing comes easy and certainly nothing comes free. She was teaching me principles I would need later in life.

Most of my years with the Caravans are filled with wonderful memories, some quite comical. I remember one incident in particular that occurred during one of our performances at the Apollo Theater. Several groups were scheduled to sing that night, each with an allocated time slot of twenty to thirty minutes. We knew that we did not have time to go through our whole routine, so we moved right into the heart of our performance. Wigs were in style at the time, and we were all wearing them. I can't remember the song our group was singing that caused such a spiritual frenzy in the auditorium, but I do know that it wiped out Delores Washington to the extent that, as she began to praise the Lord, her wig came completely off! Instantly she turned her back to the audience, held her head down, while putting both hands on top of her head as if she was trying to cover it, and continued to praise the Lord. All of a sudden with her hands raised in a gesture of praise she fell out on the floor. I must admit that we were all just as spiritually overcome as Delores, but thanks be to God we held on to our wigs! Albertina beckoned to two young men who were standing in the wings to come and take Delores off stage. One of them picked up her wig and put it under his arm as they were carrying her out. They took Delores backstage and laid her on a table. She was lying there, her eyes closed, her wig missing, hair combed straight back, yet praising the Lord and shouting, "Hallelujah, hallelujah. Thank You, Jesus." Suddenly, as if awakened from a deep sleep, she opened one eye, and said, "Where's my wig?"

I said, "Girl, get up," and we both fell out laughing.

On another occasion, we were in concert at a huge Baptist Church in Hartford, Connecticut. I could tell immediately after the very first song that the people had come to really enjoy an evening in concert with the Caravans. We had already gone through our routine—Albertina had energized the audience with the song "To Whom Shall I Turn," Cassietta George had sung "Walk Around Heaven All Day," Inez had called "Mary, Don't You Weep" to the extent that you could almost visualize Lazarus getting up out of the grave, and finally I had sung "Sweeping Through the City." Each song had seemingly reached the ultimate level of praise, and we thought we had come to the conclusion of the program, until James Herndon began to play the introduction to the song "Lord Keep Me Day by Day." Following his leading, Albertina walked to the microphone and began singing, as we joined in with her:

> *Lord, keep me day by day*
> *in a pure and perfect way.*
> *I want to live, I want to live*
> *in a building not made by hand.*
> *I'm just a stranger here,*
> *traveling through this barren land.*
> *Lord, I know, I know there is a building somewhere,*
> *a building not made by hand.*

As the spirit of God continued to move, we sang these verses over and over again. The longer we sang, the more the people shouted, and a crescendo of praise swept over the congregation. After about twenty minutes, things seemed to be simmering down, and we took our seats on a long padded bench, which was positioned to the right of the pulpit. With our eyes closed, arms folded, and swaying back and forth, we continued to sing,

I want to live, I want to live
in a building not made by hand.

All of a sudden Inez Andrews shouted out with a loud voice, "Yes, suh!" Simultaneously, she threw both of her arms outward, knocking Albertina from the bench to the floor. When she hit the floor she kept rolling like a ball until she landed down behind the piano, which was at the edge of the pulpit. There she lay, wedged between the edge of the pulpit and the side of the piano. Poor Tina! I wonder why it is that when someone falls it always seems funny to you, that is, until the shoe is on your foot. I walked over to Tina, laughingly, and asked her, "Can you get up?" She said, "No, I'm stuck. Tell Paul to come over here and help me." She was referring to Paul Foster, one of the lead singers of the Soul Stirrers who was there that night. When I think of this incident now, all I can think of is the lady in the commercial who says, "I've fallen and I can't get up!"

All of our joy rolled down behind that piano with Tina. The spirit of laughter had replaced the spirit of joy we had been feeling a few moments earlier. Delores Washington walked over and looked down at Tina. She was laughing so hard she was literally crying. "Oh, Tina," she cried.

"Shirley, what am I going to do?" Albertina asked. I said,

"Here, take my handkerchief, put it over your face and when we get you out, get up like you're praising the Lord, and the audience will think you are still in the Spirit, then just walk on out." Paul Foster came over to help her, but each time he tried to pull her up, she would holler, "Wait a minute, my foot is stuck!" At last we succeeded in freeing her, and as she walked out, she did cover her face with my handkerchief to hide her embarrassment. And, yes, the program had finally come to a conclusion!

I recall the fun times more than the difficult ones. However, the difficult times were there. The worst part of those years was the loneliness I experienced from being away from home because I missed Mama and my brothers and sisters. I also missed worshiping at my church, and fellowshiping with my friends.

To minimize my loneliness I went home every chance I got. Airfare between Chicago and Raleigh/Durham at the time was only forty-five dollars. Those trips home were special times for me—times to enjoy the haven of home, times to be with Mama, times that provided me with the opportunity to reconnect with my roots, times to recharge my spiritual batteries and to escape the perils of life that I discovered on the road.

In Durham we didn't hear much about robberies, murders, and other adverse happenings. Those things were rare where I grew up, but they were common news in Chicago and in many of the major cities where we traveled. In my travels I witnessed a lot of things that I had never encountered, such as vulgarity, immorality, and corruption.

On the other hand there were a lot of positive aspects of traveling on the road. One thing I particularly enjoyed was being able to perform with the Caravans on television. A remarkable gentleman named Sid Ordower hosted one such program, *Jubilee Showcase*. From time to time many gospel artists, such as Alex Bradford, Marion Williams, the Stars of Faith, the Soul Stirrers, James Cleveland, and the Caravans would prerecord thirty-minute shows that would be telecast later. Thanks to Sid Ordower, those videos still exist today.

In March 1997 while on tour with Vy Higginsen's Broadway musical, *Born to Sing*, we were performing in Chicago at the Chicago Theater, and Sid Ordower was in the audience. After the show, he came backstage. This was the first time I had seen him in over twenty years. He shared with me that all of those videos we had taped on *Jubilee Showcase*, which numbered in the hundreds, are in the archives of Mayor Harold Washington's library in Chicago. He also informed me that the tapes will never leave the library, but will always be available for big-screen viewing by the public, including all students. I consider it a phenomenal blessing that gospel music has been preserved in such a profound manner. Great artists such as Bessie Griffin, Sally Martin, Brother Joe Mays, Dorothy Love Coates and the Original Gospel Harmonettes, the Davis Sisters, and others will forever be with us on tape because of Sid Ordower, and I just want to say to him, "Thank you."

While meeting with Sid that night after the performance, and listening to him as he talked enthusiastically about the tapes, I could actually see the joy on his face as he expressed what having them meant. I thought to myself, Here is a man with a mission. God had entrusted him with a ministry to preserve an art form that gave purpose and meaning to millions of lives, and he had accomplished that charge. Gospel music owes a debt of gratitude to Sid Ordower. Personally, I will be eternally thankful to Sid and to the Caravans. They both helped to establish me in my present ministry.

During the time that I was a member, the Caravans were one of the most well-known groups on the gospel scene. In our traveling to share the gospel of Jesus Christ in song, the Lord always blessed us in all our efforts. And as He blessed us, we always remembered to bless those who were less fortunate. We never lost sight of the fact that it was the Lord who was blessing us and that all glory belonged to Him.

I came to the Caravans a very naive young girl, straight out of bobby socks, quite impetuous, and extremely unaware. But Albertina and the other group members took me under their care and taught me practical living—things like how to drive, how to interact with people, how to budget my money, and how to enhance my singing. They demonstrated poise that I could emulate and protected me from the dangers of the road. I will always be indebted to them for all the wonderful things they taught me.

They were also my protectors and guardians when I began dating. They would often tell me, "Because you are new on the road, you must be watchful."

I admit, I was a little nervous about dating. In fact, I was very apprehensive about almost everything. After all, I had only traveled a small area of the Southeast before joining the Caravans. I was coming from under the wings of my mother and from the shelter of my church family. I hadn't thought much about dating because, usually, I stayed so busy I didn't have much time for socializing. However, from time to time, on an off day, I would accept an invitation to dinner.

I remember one of the funniest dates I ever had. Traveling as I did, I never had a chance to really learn how to cook very well. While my other sisters had spent a great deal of time observing and learning from Mama in the kitchen, I just never had the opportunity to do so.

One night I had invited this young man over for dinner, and one of the items on my menu was homemade biscuits. A few days earlier, a friend of mine, Mary Davis Robinson, had taught me how to bake biscuits from scratch, and I wanted to try the recipe out on somebody.

Trying to remember what she had shown me, I threw a few ingredients together (some flour, water, salt, baking powder, and butter), pinched out the dough, rolled it up into circular biscuits, patted them in a pan, and slipped them into the oven.

When I took them out, they were a bit crusty at the edges and much larger and whiter than the ones Mary had made. They resembled an old-fashioned hoe cake but not too bad, I thought.

We sat down to eat, and my date picked up a biscuit to put it in his mouth. As he did so, it crumbled in his hands, breaking into a million pieces, as fine and powdery as a handful of beach sand all over his shirt and pants. Obviously, I had put too much baking powder in the recipe! I wanted to be embarrassed, but it was just so funny. We couldn't quit laughing about those biscuits. The evening was not a total loss. After we regained our composure from laughing about the biscuits, I quickly drove to the store, bought a loaf of bread, came back, and continued with the evening. Eventually, I did learn to cook, but not like my mom. Before my culinary skills improved I can remember baking turkey wings for twenty-four hours and cooking collard greens for twenty minutes. I have definitely improved since then.

My years with the Caravans were an invaluable educational experience. I learned a great deal about music. I was taught by the best, for every last one of the members of the Caravans possessed great musical gifts. Everyone was a lead singer. They were considered an all-star group.

Over the years, each member of the group—Albertina Walker, Inez Andrews, Delores Washington, Cassietta George, Josephine Howard, and myself—could and did take lead vocals in our concerts. Even our keyboard players—James Herndon and Eddie Williams—were also powerful vocalists. We really didn't have a first and second tier of singers. Everyone was first-rate.

After I left the Caravans, everyone else eventually went solo and succeeded in their careers. Those years gave a young, untested singer like myself the opportunity to learn technique and musicianship.

Those years allowed me the opportunity to meet and learn from scores of other gospel artists whose styles I admired. One of the greatest events of my life was meeting Mahalia Jackson, the most anointed and awesome female gospel artist of our time. I remember I became so excited when I first saw her that I yelled, "That's Mahalia Jackson!" and ran across the vestibule of the church where we were singing and threw my arms around her. Somehow, in the middle of her surprise, she embraced me, not knowing at all who I was or what I was doing.

Later, Albertina cautioned me about being so impulsive. She said it made me seem overly anxious and unprofessional. I always took everything Albertina told me to heart. But that was one time I didn't listen to her. I didn't care if I seemed awestruck. I was.

Mahalia Jackson was the greatest, the true Queen of Gospel Music, and I felt honored to meet her.

The Caravans were my mentors, my sisters, my friends, and my family. We disagreed some, cried some, laughed a lot, and poured out our hearts onstage and in churches for the glory of God. I learned from them all and believe even today that I sing a little like each of them. I would like to think that I have a little bit of their styles in my music.

Instinctively I knew when it was time to leave the Caravans and to move into my own ministry. I didn't plan on it happening, but I felt the continuous prompting and urging of the Lord to move into another realm of ministry. Up until that point I had been singing the melody of the gospel, but now I was distinctively hearing God's voice to expound the word of the gospel.

The events that led to the end of my time with the Caravans happened without any prearranged planning on anybody's part. I guess that made it easier. It was all about God's timing. I was saddened, but I knew the move was God's perfect will for my life, and therefore I knew I would be okay, even if it meant that I had to leave the comfortable and the familiar for the scary and the unknown.

CHAPTER SIX
On My Own

THE MELODY

I'll go . . . I'll go . . . I'll go
If the Lord needs somebody,
here am I, O Lord, send me.

I may be motherless, but I'll go
I may be motherless, but I'll go
If the Lord needs somebody,
here am I, O Lord, send me.

I may be fatherless, but I'll go
I may be fatherless, but I'll go
If the Lord needs somebody,
here am I, O Lord, send me.
    —"I'll Go"

AND THE WORD

And see, now I go bound in the spirit to Jerusalem,
not knowing the things that will happen to me there.
    —Acts 20:22

ALTHOUGH it's not easy, I'm not one to avoid making crucial decisions. And one of the most difficult decisions I have ever had to make in my life was deciding to leave the Caravans. After all, they had been a part of my life for eight years, and had become as dear to me as my own family. Traveling and singing as a member of the Caravans was one of my greatest joys. I honestly didn't want to leave, but in my spirit I knew that God was leading me into an ecclesiastical ministry.

For months I wrestled with the idea, fasting, praying, wanting to be sure that this contemplated move was the Lord's perfect will for my life. Earnestly seeking Him, I repeatedly asked, "Lord, is there any other way?" In response, I kept hearing His voice speaking to my spirit, urging me, compelling me, drawing me, calling me into a separate ministry.

Singing for the Lord had always been my passion, but at the age of seventeen, before I joined the Caravans, the Lord had commissioned me to also proclaim His Word. I had always known that the day would come when I would have to actively work toward fulfilling that charge.

It was obvious that my remaining with the Caravans was only delaying the inevitable. As long as I stayed, I would only be able to partially fulfill God's mandate. With them, I was singing the gospel, and in our concerts people were being blessed and many were accepting Christ into their lives. But I was not fulfilling God's direct edict to evangelize His Word. Our rigorous, inflexible concert itinerary made it almost impossible for me to schedule any speaking engagements and, to a large degree, deprived me of the liberty to accept the invitations I frequently received to conduct revival services.

Albertina and I had tried countless times to remedy this situation. Together we would scrutinize our calendar, searching for weekends that were not scheduled for concerts. During those rare off times, I would accept invitations to minister at churches. However, all too often, someone would call Albertina to engage the Caravans in concert, and forgetting that she had told me the dates were free, she would accept. At the last minute, I would have to cancel the revival service.

Over the years, this frequently happened. Albertina didn't purposely create this problem. She was only trying to fulfill her obligation to the Caravans. After all, she was responsible for the welfare of the entire group, and her first priority was to keep us working. I understood. But, on the other hand, every canceled revival made me acutely aware of the fact that I had failed to keep a commitment, both to God and to the church I had disappointed. Although, in essence, the scheduling conflicts weren't my fault, they bothered me. My mother's words would reverberate in my mind, "Shirley Ann, your word is all you have; you don't make promises that you can't keep." I knew I couldn't continue in that manner. I had to pursue what my heart, mind, and spirit were dictating. If the Lord was really leading me, I would succeed. If not, I would fail. Either way, I had to try.

There were also other circumstances that contributed to my leaving the Caravans. A recording company, Hob Records, approached me with a contract offer to record on their label. At the time Albertina was the only one out of our group that was signed with a record company. She was under contract with Savoy Records, the most noted gospel label in the industry. Although this was Albertina's individual contract agreement with Savoy, we recorded with her under the nomenclature "Albertina Walker and the Caravans."

Therefore when Hob Records offered me four thousand dollars as a signing bonus to record for them, I just knew that she would understand what a wonderful career opportunity this could be for me. The Caravans were always a closely knit group; we were a sisterhood. We functioned as a unit, based upon a one-for-all-and-all-for-one concept. So naturally when I received the offer, my first thoughts were of how I could include Albertina, Inez, and Delores. I went to Albertina and said, "Tina, here's what I propose. I would like to sign with Hob Records and share the advance royalty, keeping two thousand dollars for myself and giving the group two thousand dollars to divide among themselves."

To my surprise, she said no. By allowing me to accept an independent record deal, she felt that it might split the group, causing the others to do the same, if given the opportunity. Here I was caught between a rock and a hard place. I didn't know what to do. I loved working with the Caravans, but I also knew that the Lord was expanding my career and ministry into new domains. Again, I began to pray, "Lord, what should I do?"

Often when we come to a point where we don't know what to do, the Lord will send prevailing circumstances to navigate us in the direction of His will. That is exactly what happened.

It was time for Albertina to record her next project with Savoy and, as always, we were scheduled to record with her. I had been in Long Island, but we had agreed that I would meet them at the Cecil Hotel where they would be lodging in New York City. The day of the recording I called the hotel continuously, but I didn't get an answer. No one was in their room. I didn't know what to think. I knew the time of the recording was approximately 2:30 in the afternoon, but I didn't know the name or the address of the studio. I kept calling and calling the hotel. Finally, Inez Andrews answered the telephone and told me that Albertina and the others had gone to Newark, New Jersey, to record the album without me. For a period of time, Inez had resigned from the Caravans to pursue a solo career, and during that interim she had signed with a recording label. She eventually returned to the Caravans, but she was still under contract, and the terms of the agreement precluded her from recording with the group that day.

I was disappointed and hurt that Albertina and the group had chosen to record without me, but to be very honest I was not angry because deep in my heart I felt that God was working out the situation. Now, in retrospect, when I think about the whole situation, I know that everything that happened was all a part of God's master plan working in my behalf.

Having resolved in my mind to leave the Caravans, I approached Albertina with my decision. That was one of the hardest things I have ever had to do. For eight years, Albertina and the Caravans had been my family. She had been like a mother to me, and I valued and respected her judgment. But I could no longer disobey the Lord. We were performing at the Apollo Theater in New York City when I told her my decision. Arriving at the theater, I went immediately upstairs to our dressing room. Hanging up my coat, I told Albertina that I would be resigning. "I have a charge to keep," I said, "and that charge is to the Lord." She didn't try to talk me out of it. In a way, I wanted her to, but she didn't. She just shrugged her shoulders a little and said, "Okay, if that's what you want."

I could tell that she was deeply hurt, and so was I. But because the Lord was controlling the situation from beginning to ending, we departed friends and have remained the best of friends to this day. Whatever hurt we may have felt then has completely dissipated. The reason I know this to be true is because whenever one calls for the others, we drop everything and come running.

Being the wise woman that she is, I think Albertina knew

that it was time for my tenure with the Caravans to end. Although she didn't say it, she seemed to understand that in order for me to keep growing spiritually, I needed to pursue my ministry according to God's will.

I performed my last concert with the Caravans in August of 1966—the same month I had joined them, eight years earlier.

On my own, I now had the flexibility to coordinate the scheduling of my concerts around my revival dates. Having that freedom was liberating. I no longer felt as if I was failing the Lord. But on the other hand, I soon discovered how difficult traveling alone and performing solo concerts could be. I had no support, no booking agent, no secretary, no background singers, and no musicians. I didn't even have a keyboard player. It was literally Jesus and me.

At times, this became a little embarrassing, particularly when the sponsor of the concert would have to ask over the PA system if anyone in the auditorium could play the piano. Someone would either raise their hand or shout out from the audience, and that volunteer would be my musician for the evening. Sometimes they were accomplished musicians, and often they were mediocre, but I have always believed that some music is better than no music.

Many times I would check into a hotel and order room service, and while eating dinner alone, I would invariably imagine that I could hear the members of the Caravans talking down the hall or in the next room. I had been with them so long, I could almost hear them saying, "Hey, can I borrow a pair of stockings?" or "Girl, I need some toothpaste." I would laugh as I imagined their voices, and then cry when I realized they weren't really there. I missed them so much!

Often, I would simply sit in my hotel room and cry. It was during those low times that I found myself asking, "Lord,

At age eight I was already singing for Jesus in local churches in North and South Carolina.

My father's singing group, The Just Come Four Quartet. Left to right: S. B. Brown, second tenor; M. W. Williams, first tenor; J. S. Caesar, first bass; and E. L. Gibson, second bass.

I sang with Lucius Leroy Johnson as "Baby Shirley" when I was twelve. Here we receive an award.

Singing with the Caravans at age twenty-two. Left to right: Myself, Cassietta George, James Herndon, singer and manager Albertina Walker, Josephine Howard, and Inez Andrews.

The Shirley Caesar Singers on Jubilee Showcase in 1972. The group at the right is the Spencer Jackson Family.

A publicity picture of Shirley Caesar and the Shirley Caesar Singers taken in 1973. From left to right: James Jones, my sister Anne Price, Barbara Amos, Suella Colbert, myself, and Bernard Sterling.

Pictures from an early
concert of the Shirley
Caesar Singers.

The "Electrifying Evangelist" in 1975.

With Andrew Young in my dressing room at the Civic Center in Atlanta, Georgia, before a concert in 1984.

Bishop Harold Williams and I open a present at our wedding on June 26, 1984.

Oh, happy day! After going back to college, I finally receive my B.S.
degree in business administration from Shaw University in May of 1984.

President and Mrs. Carter host a gospel singing event on the White House lawn on September 9, 1979. The president said he was a fan who had several of my albums. Here we all enjoy this decorative artifact.

My husband, Harold, and me with President Bush, February 19, 1992, at a White House event. I sang, and Maya Angelou read some of her poetry.

Oh, my Grammy! This one for "He's Working It Out for You" in 1993.

Jazz singer Nancy Wilson and I pose with my Living Legend Award given in memory of Dr. Martin Luther King Jr. on January 16, 1995, at the American Music Industry Political Action Committee.

ELECT

SHIRLEY CAESAR

for

City Council

AT-LARGE

PULL LEVER

9A

S h i r l e y
C a e s a r

Shirley Caesar is more than just a Gospel Singer

(Paid for by the Committee to Elect Shirley Caesar to City Council)

My campaign publicity for the
Durham City Council in 1985.
My motto: Shirley Caesar is
more than just a gospel singer.

I pay a visit to a family who has received economic assistance through the
Shirley Caesar Outreach Ministries: Nettie Fewel (holding the child), her
husband, Kenneth (right rear), and their six children.

Pastor Shirley Caesar of the Mount Calvary Word of Faith Church in Raleigh, North Carolina.

The 24th Annual Conference of the Shirley Caesar Ministries at Fayetteville, North Carolina, in 1996. Left to right: my manager, Carolyn Sanders, Society of European State Authors and Composers executive Norman Odlum, myself, and my husband.

First lady Hillary Rodham Clinton and myself at the National Federation of Black Women Business Luncheon in Washington, D.C. I sang for the occasion, which honored Mrs. Clinton.

The Shirley Caesar Singers with President Bill Clinton and Vice President Al Gore at the Women's Leadership Forum, Washington, D.C., in June of 1996. Left to right: President Clinton, myself, Carolyn Sanders, Carolyn's niece, Amanda, Bernard Amanda, Bernard Sterling, Lisa Butts, my sister Anne Price, Vice President Gore, Linda Conyers Nix, and Gene Conyers.

did I make the right decision?" Prior to leaving the Caravans, I talked to Clara Ward, a well-known gospel singer, about what I was contemplating. She encouraged me to stay with them. "You have been with them and have helped to build this fire," she said. "It's not the time to leave. If I were you, I would stay there and keep warm by that fire."

I told her, "The Lord called me to ministry."

She said, "You can do that anytime."

That first year, I wondered if she was right. The most difficult time came at the end of that first summer. I was performing a concert in Columbus, Ohio. The weather was extremely hot, and the air was stifling. As I waited behind the curtain to go onstage in that small auditorium with no air-conditioning, I was perspiring in the heat. I wanted to begin my performance, but again, the master of ceremonies had to ask for a volunteer to play keyboard for me. As he did, an overwhelming sense of embarrassment engulfed me. I couldn't continue in this manner. I had to find a way to establish my own group. I needed help on the road. I wanted someone to travel with me.

That night, after the concert, I called my mother in Durham. "Mama, do you think Anne could come and help me?"

At the time, my sister Anne was singing in nightclubs in, and around, Fayetteville, North Carolina, making twenty dollars a night. When I talked to her, I told her I would give her a hundred dollars per concert just to come on the road to be my companion, my company keeper, my friend. I felt like the apostle Paul writing to Timothy, asking him to join him as he traveled preaching the gospel.

Within a few days, Anne joined me, and having her with me made all the difference in the world.

Other gospel artists on the road encouraged me, including the Five Blind Boys of Alabama, Clarence Fountain, Johnny

Fields, and J. J. Farley of the Soul Stirrers. They told me to hang in there, that I had what it took to make it. From time to time, I even ran into the Caravans.

After Anne began traveling with me, things gradually began to improve. Within a short time I acquired my first keyboard player, Johnny (Rainey) Griffin. I needed background singers, but I didn't have the money to pay any, so I improvised. At times I utilized church choirs where we were performing, and at other times I managed to save enough money to pay a choir for one or two performances.

Two years after leaving the Caravans, the Lord sent two background singers to join my group. They were Linda Martin and Donna Jones from Dayton, Ohio. Now with Anne, Rainey, Linda, and Donna, I finally had the group I needed. They became the original Caesar Singers who accompanied me on both concerts and revivals.

The security of having my own group was wonderful, but with that security came a great deal of responsibility. Each of them was depending on me for their living; therefore, I had to make sure I secured enough concert dates to generate the revenue needed to pay them.

On one occasion, I learned a lesson about responsibility in a manner that I would have preferred to avoid. We had just performed a concert in Wichita, Kansas, pouring our hearts and souls into the service as always. Afterward, I searched for the promoter to receive our compensation. But he was nowhere to be found. He had left without paying us!

I was perplexed. Why had he done such a thing? Why had he taken advantage of us? I didn't have the answers, but I was going to find out. Determined and disappointed, I found out where he lived and went to his house. I knocked, but he wouldn't come to the door. I later called, but he wouldn't answer the telephone. I did everything I knew to do, but he wouldn't talk to me. I didn't have any money saved for such emergencies, and I knew the others needed to be paid. Guilt overshadowed me. How could I have let this occur? Surely there must have been something I could have done to safeguard against this happening. All I could think of was the fact that my group had depended on me to take care of business matters, and I had failed. The promoter later called and apologized, but he never paid the money he owed us.

I wish I could say that was the only time that type of situation has happened to us, but it wasn't. On another occasion we were scheduled to perform a concert that had ten other groups on the program. We were last on the billing. As each group prepared to go onstage the promoter paid them, but when it came our turn to perform, there wasn't any money to pay us. The promoter had again left the auditorium and was nowhere to be found. The other groups kept telling me not to sing. They said, "I would not sing, if I were you. Just go out there and tell the audience the promoter left without paying you, and if you sing you can't pay your group." My group members were sitting there wondering what I was going to do. We could hear the audience clapping and chanting, "We want Shirley. We want Shirley." Over the roar of the audience, in my mind I could hear my mother saying, "Shirley, the people are depending on you, don't you ever let them down, and don't ever let God down." I knew that whether or not we were paid, we had to minister in song to God's people. When people came to us after the concert telling us how much they had been blessed, and how God had touched their hearts as we sang, we were more than adequately compensated. Over the years I have learned to take such incidents in stride. They happen, and try as I might I am not able to prevent them. My priority is to ensure that I have done what the Lord has told me to do.

There have been times when I have only received enough money to pay the group members without anything left for myself. But I was okay with that, because I felt that I was at least able to fulfill my obligation to them, and I knew the Lord would take care of me. And He did.

I must admit that once I became the manager of my own group, I readily understood why Albertina felt that group members signing individual record contracts would destroy the continuity of the group. When a key member of the Caesar Singers did just that without my knowledge, I experienced firsthand the breach it caused within the structure of the group. No longer were we a single unit because now his priorities had changed. His commitment and loyalty to the group were minimal as he focused on his personal career.

It disrupted our performance because often he missed our engagements to fulfill his own concert schedule. As usual Albertina had been right. I couldn't see it then, but now I could.

But that experience taught me a valuable lesson. No longer do I totally depend on group members. Everyone is free to pursue their own career goals. They are at liberty to work for my group or on any other job. They all function as independent contractors. If I'm scheduled for a concert and they are available I will use them. If not, I'll go in the strength of the Lord.

The Caesar Singers were a great group to travel with on the road. The good times far outweighed the bad. We were a family. The same bond I experienced with the Caravans was present among us. We prayed together, we cried together, and we laughed together. I remember our first appearance in Disneyland. We were performing the song "No Charge" and part of the rendition was to dramatize Jesus being nailed to the cross. With his arms outstretched, Bernard Sterling, one of my singers, portrayed Jesus on the cross, as I symbolically hammered the nails in his hands with the microphone. Totally immersed in the song, I proceeded to demonstrate how Jesus' feet were nailed to the cross. As I bowed, I received the shock of my life. Bernard was wearing big, floppy Mickey Mouse shoes! I was taken completely by surprise. I lost my concentration. All I wanted to do was laugh! I didn't think I would be able to finish the song, but somehow I did. Bernard later explained that he had left his shoes at home and didn't realize it until the last minute, too late to purchase any before the concert.

The sadness of leaving the Caravans began to pass with the years. My evangelism ministry was steadily expanding. I was conducting as many revivals as I was performing concerts. The Lord was opening doors across the country. Again, I was offered the opportunity to record with Hob Records. This time I accepted. The title of my first solo album was *I'll Go*. To me, it was reaffirmation that God indeed keeps His promises.

From my days with the Caravans to the present, I have seen a complete revolution in the recording of gospel music. It has evolved from the small mom-and-pop studios with a shoestring budget, to the mega forty-eight-track studios and huge production budgets. When I recorded with the Caravans, the production budgets were always very meager. There weren't any allocations to hire musicians. Often we borrowed musicians from local churches. At best we had a drummer, a bass, a lead guitarist, and an organ player. We couldn't afford to pay for studio time for more than one day, so we would record ten to twelve songs in one session. If we made mistakes, the producer overlooked them. If the altos came in late or the sopranos didn't sing the song as rehearsed, it was ignored because the budget would not allow rerecording.

Today, of course, recordings require months of intricate planning and development. Songs have to be written or chosen and rehearsed, musicians must be acquired, coproducers have to be named, and studios have to be selected. We are usually in the studio from morning until late at night, for several days. It does not matter whether we are singing one line, five lines, or the whole song. Our main endeavor is to record it perfectly. We use instruments of all kinds—violins, saxophones, synthesizers—you name it. If someone makes a mistake, you fix it. You record it over and over and over again, until you get it right.

Personally, I prefer live recordings rather than studio recordings. The required preparation is greater, but I love the excitement and the energy I receive from the audience. For live recordings I work closely with my record company in choosing the venue and the choir. (I always prefer recording in a church because the presence of the Lord is there.) The choirs we choose, for the most part, predetermine the cities where the recordings will take place. For instance, with my last album, *A Miracle in Harlem*, we chose Hezekiah Walker and the Love Fellowship Choir, therefore the recording session was held in New York City where they are located.

The day before the recording session, Joe Neal of Doppler Studios in Atlanta, Georgia, arrived in a truck with all the recording paraphernalia—tapes, sound equipment, and a sophisticated recording board. The studio was brought on wheels to the church. Right before the live session Bubba Smith, my coproducer, went out to coach the audience; in a sense, he got them ready to receive what the Lord had given me for the evening. He said, "I want you to give me the biggest applause you can give me." Then he had them give out a great shout as they applauded. These sound effects were all recorded for use in later editing and mixing in case the applause after each song was not as loud or broad as we liked.

Yes, gospel music has certainly arrived. Today, it ranks with country, classical, and jazz in both sales (close to one billion) and fans. Gospel is a world in itself. In fact, it is so immense that many of the secular artists, such as Aretha Franklin, Whitney Houston (with whom I had the privilege of recording "He's All Over Me" on *The Preacher's Wife* soundtrack), and Patti LaBelle are returning to their roots and again recording gospel.

I thank God for the paths I have traveled in life, for the lean years because they taught me patience, and for the prosperous years because they demonstrated God's faithfulness. Although there were some difficult times in those early days after leaving the Caravans that caused me to wonder if I had made the right decision, I am so glad that I trusted the Lord and followed His leading. If I had not, I would never have realized the full scope of my ministry.

CHAPTER SEVEN

Forgive and Forget

THE MELODY

Forgive and forget
That is the way Christians ought to live
Leaving the past behind
Forgive and forget.

Jesus died for your sins and mine
Never to remember them again
Oh, if you want to go higher, higher in Jesus
Leave the past behind.

Forgive and forget
That is the way Christians ought to live
Leaving the past behind
Forgive and forget
—"Forgive and Forget"

⸿⸿⸿⸿⸿⸿⸿⸿ AND THE WORD ⸿⸿⸿⸿⸿⸿⸿⸿

There is neither Jew nor Greek,
there is neither slave nor free,
there is neither male nor female;
for you are all one in Christ Jesus.
—Galatians 3:28

THE day of April 4, 1968, stands out in the mind of every African American. Certainly those alive at the time will never forget it. That was the day James Earl Ray shot and murdered Dr. Martin Luther King Jr. as he stood on the balcony of the Lorraine Hotel in Memphis, Tennessee. I had stayed in that hotel many times, and quite possibly in that very room. I can remember, even now, where I was and what I was doing when I heard the news.

I was in the car with my group driving across Ohio, en route to a concert. The first of the spring buds on the trees had begun to bloom, and a warm breeze cut through the air. We were all in a good mood, enjoying the sunshine that reflected through the car window, and the sounds of music coming from the radio.

Then we heard the news. The announcer interrupted the radio program to make a special announcement. I leaned forward to listen, wondering what tragic news was about to be revealed. Violence and bloodshed on almost every hand marked that era in our country. But, even with that knowledge, I was not prepared for what I heard next. I couldn't believe my ears! *Dr. Martin Luther King Jr. had been shot in Memphis, Tennessee, and he was dead.*

For the most part, I try to refrain from talking about the

negative things of life and accentuate the positive, but some things just can't be ignored. As a young black woman trying to overcome adversity and accomplish a music career in the sixties, I certainly could not ignore the racial tensions that tore at the edges of America. Like all African Americans, I had to deal with racism, and it wasn't easy. More times than not, I wondered what would happen to us, how would the Shirley Caesar Singers make it on the road during this time of racism.

One night the seven of us were in a waffle shop in Georgia. We were just sitting, eating, and minding our own business when two white men came in and looked around. One of them commented to the other very loudly, "My, isn't it dark in here tonight." Had I not instilled in our group the principle *We don't fight our own battles, but God fights for us,* there's no telling what would have happened. There were a couple of members in our group who were not totally delivered and who in all probability would have said something in retaliation. But instead we simply held our peace, finished eating, got up, and left.

Growing up in the South, the problems of racism and other prejudices affected me as they did all African Americans. They operated in my city and in my community, and I experienced them both firsthand. As a result, I hate prejudice and racism more than I hate anything else in the world. They are terrible, destructive forces. I learned long ago that prejudice and racism aren't the same. *Prejudice* doesn't necessarily have anything to do with a person's race. *Racism,* by the very meaning of the word, obviously does.

As a teenager in high school, I experienced the sting of *prejudice* from one of my teachers who formed an opinion of me that was totally unwarranted. She somehow surmised that I was not college material and that I definitely should not entertain the thought of furthering my education beyond high school. In her words she told me, "Girl, you will be wasting your mother's money if you spend it on college. You're just not college material." Her prejudice against me certainly was not based upon my academic performance, because I maintained a strong *B* average in her class throughout the year.

Perhaps she didn't like it that some Monday mornings, after I had traveled and sung all weekend, performing as many as three concerts on Sunday alone, I would come to her class late, tired, sleepy, and, oh, I might add a bit irritable. She didn't take into consideration that my traveling on weekends was necessary to help my mother support our family. Neither did she consider my determination to be in school as opposed to staying home after such a strenuous weekend. Often I didn't arrive home until 3:00 or 4:00 in the morning and had to be in school by 8:30. I may have been late, but I never missed a day in any class. I kept up with the course work and excelled academically. I admit that I was late so often that they used to call me Shirley "late" Caesar. Perhaps that teacher, whose name I won't call, had the right to be upset with me coming to her class late, but she did not have the right to prejudge my intellect or my future. I'm glad I didn't listen to her. When I think of her, I think of a prejudiced person. She wasn't a racist (she was an African American, just like me), but she had a preconceived low esteem of me, and it was obvious she wasn't going to change. That teacher's perspective of me became a challenge, and I resolved to continue my education to prove her wrong. Although I had to initially drop out of college because I didn't have the money to continue, I was determined at some point to return and earn my degree. That resolve became a reality in 1981 when I enrolled at Shaw University in Raleigh, North Carolina, and in 1984 I graduated magna cum laude with a degree in business administration. When I held that degree in my hand, I felt that I had finally proven that teacher wrong. Although I turned her words into a challenge, another student, less determined than myself, might have easily given up, dropped out of school never to return, and ended up a criminal or a drug addict.

Prejudice can be harmful in that manner. Prejudice occurs any time that one person enters a situation where another person has already prejudged his actions and his capabilities. Prejudice occurs when a person sees a woman in the pulpit and automatically concludes she should not be there, regardless of her anointing or the fact that the Lord has called her to that ministry. Prejudice occurs when a teacher prejudges a student as a slow learner, when a rich person looks down on a poor person, or when a slim person humiliates a heavy person.

Make no mistake about it. Prejudice cuts both ways. If a black person automatically sees a white person as mean or evil, simply because of their skin color, that's prejudice. When a woman automatically thinks every man is against her, that's prejudice. When a person of one political party automatically disagrees with a person of another, that's prejudice. Unfortunately, prejudice is an undeniable part of our society. The larger category of prejudice, of course, includes the awful existence of racism.

As a little girl in Durham, I initially wasn't aware of racism. Like most children, I just went about my business, playing with my friends, going to church, and spending time at home and in the neighborhood. I recognized that when we went to town I drank at different water fountains from the whites and used different rest rooms (if any were made available at all). But all of that was commonplace, and I didn't go to town often enough for it to have any significant bearing on me. Other than our infrequent trips to town, I didn't have much contact with anyone other than black people. From time to time, I heard other people talking about one thing or another in terms of race relations, but nothing was dramatic enough to influence me in forming an opinion about other racial groups.

In the South during those Jim Crow days, ethnic groups were for the most part segregated, with the blacks residing in one part of town and the whites in the other. Blacks left the neighborhood in the daytime to work for or with white people, but other than that, the two racial lines didn't cross that much. When I began school, I noticed something that made me aware that things were very different for blacks than whites. It wasn't anything dramatic, but in my child's mind, the incident mattered. It centered on cookies—that's right, cookies.

At first I thought that Mrs. Davis, a white lady, was just plain mean. But gradually I understood that her problem was much deeper. She didn't hate everybody, just black people. She operated a small convenience store three blocks from our house, and every day after school all the kids went by her store. We called it Mrs. Davis's store. In the backyard of her store she built a fence, and one side faced the black community. There was so much hatred in her heart, that she painted the side that faced us black. The other side was white.

In Mrs. Davis's store there were always two jars of cookies on the counter, one stale and the other fresh. She habitually sold us the stale cookies or the chocolate candy that had been there for weeks, possibly with worms in it. The fresh cookies were only sold to the white children. In my child's mind, it was obvious to me that this lady did not like black children.

On one occasion my friends and I went into her store after school to buy some candy. Like most kids, we were playing around, talking loud, and laughing. Nothing harmful, just regular kid stuff. Mrs. Davis got upset with us. She said, "If you all don't get out of here, I'm going to call the police." She would call us names, like the *n* word or monkeys, and she would watch us as if we were in there to take something from her. Of course, that wasn't why we were there, and we never stole anything from her.

I have always believed that when you sow good seeds, good will come back to you. And if you sow bad seeds, you are going to reap bad seeds. Something horrible happened to Mrs. Davis. Tragically, weeks later, in the Durham newspaper, we read that someone had broken into her store, robbed her, beaten her up, and put her in the store refrigerator. Thankfully, the robber didn't kill her. The guilty person was a white man.

Even though she treated us badly, I didn't want her hurt. To want that would mean I had descended to her level and had become as racist as she was. Mrs. Davis had racial problems. She must have been very unhappy in her life. I believe that some good is in the very worst of us and that some bad is in even the best of us. All of us have faults, and revenge doesn't make sense.

After the incidents surrounding Mrs. Davis, I began noticing other things. When we went to a restaurant, we couldn't sit in certain places or they wouldn't serve us at all. When we went to the movies, we had to go in the back door and sit in the balcony. We lived in neighborhoods where some of the roads were unpaved and most had potholes, while the whites lived in neighborhoods with paved streets and few potholes. We simply didn't venture into the white neighborhoods because we knew we were disliked and would be treated badly.

From time to time I heard the names white people used to degrade blacks. The *n* word, *ink spot, tar baby*—all those awful names. I remember people saying: "If you're black, stay back. If you're brown, stick around. If you're white, you're all right." I don't know where that sick saying came from, but it became embedded in my mind.

As I grew older, I realized that although my sisters, Anne, Lina, Virginia, Gertrude, and even my aunts, Ida and Helen, could work in the hotels downtown (and they did), they could not stay there or eat there. Although women in my neighborhood could cook and take care of the little white children and clean their homes, they were not allowed to eat in the same restaurants with them or live near them.

Without question I had grown to become quite familiar with prejudice and racism, but never was the impact felt more than during the time immediately following Dr. King's death. At the reality of Dr. King's demise, fear gripped my heart. There was the potential that his murder could provoke riots across America and thereby serve to undermine Dr. King's very mission. Still not really believing it and not sure what else to do, we immediately pulled the car over to the side of the road and sat in utter dismay. Silence filled the car for the next few minutes, and then the silence turned into weeping.

Staring out the window, I wondered how it could have happened. I admit I became very angry, but shortly thereafter, my anger subsided and sadness gripped my heart. All I could think of was Mrs. Coretta Scott King and her small children. Not knowing what else to do, I closed my eyes, bowed my head, and prayed not only for Mrs. King but also for America. I prayed that we could find a way to work through the pain and suffering that this tragedy would cause.

I felt sorry that I wouldn't have the opportunity to know Dr. King. I had shaken his hand once in Atlanta years earlier after he had spoken at the Regency Hotel, but I was one of many in a huge crowd that day.

As I prayed, I asked the Lord to remind people that Dr. King had preached love and not hate, forgiveness and not revenge, peace and not war. I prayed that somehow, out of it all, Dr. King's life would not have been in vain and that someday his dream might come true for all of us.

Over the next few days following his assassination, I listened closely to what people around me were saying. Many were filled with indignation and wanted to retaliate. They were tired of all the hatred, all the maltreatment, and all the racial inequality and wanted to do something drastic. Many were ready to get their guns and go into the streets. Others said, "No, that won't help. We must do what Dr. King would want us to do. Be peaceful. Resist, but with nonviolence and love."

People were divided on the issue of whether to take vengeance or practice Dr. King's philosophy of nonviolence, but they all agreed on one fact and repeatedly commented, "It seems like whenever there is someone who wants to help humanity and unite the people, society always destroys him."

As a minister and a gospel singer and to some degree a leader in the African-American community, I had to do some real soul searching because, in all honesty, like the majority of Black America I was hurt, bewildered, and quite upset. I kept pondering, What should my stance be? How do I respond? Should I march and protest? Should I speak out against man's inhumanity to man? I am not a proponent of violence in any form, but I wondered when I stood to minister, what could I possibly say to a world so torn apart by racial division during these dreadful times?

Coming out of a season of prayer, fasting, and careful thought, I decided I could serve the Lord best not by leading my people in marches and protests or waving banners, but by *using the pulpit and the stage to proclaim Jesus' gospel of grace and love and to reaffirm Dr. King's position of non-violence*. I resolved to help my people by preaching and teaching that we are all made in God's image and that the color of our skin is immaterial. I would let them know that in God's eyes we are all equal and that there is no person, race, or nationality that is superior to the other. I would stress that we must not be consumed by hatred and jealousy, for hate destroys the hater, and jealousy is crueler than the grave.

In my first sermon after Dr. King's death I told the congregation, "We are a blessed people in spite of everything, and the Lord will take care of us. He always has, and He always will. You don't fight hate with hate; you fight hate with love. So love those who despitefully use you, and persecute you, and speak evil against you. Don't condescend to the enemy's level. Remember that Jesus always responded to hate with love, and Dr. Martin Luther King Jr. personified the teachings of Jesus. If he were here this morning, I believe he would tell us, "'And let us not be weary in well doing: for in due season we shall reap if we faint not'" (Galatians 6:9 KJV).

Since that time I have delivered many messages that have dealt with the issue of how to respond to undeserved pain and strife. One such sermon, which I entitled "Just Let It Go," relates an incident that I personally struggled with. An individual whom I considered a friend began to spread mean, ugly untruths about me. I tried to ignore the accusations, but I was devastated. I refrained from confronting the person because I didn't want to dignify their slurs with a response, and neither did I want them to feel they could provoke me to anger. But for the life of me, I could not understand why they would try to slander and defame my character. They had experienced much pain in life as a result of having been reared in foster homes because of a broken family. I tried to be a friend. I counseled with them, prayed for them, and helped them financially, and in return they maliciously lied about me, not once or twice but repeatedly. The lies were so horrific that I actually contemplated taking the person to court for defamation of character. But then I asked myself, What would Jesus do? I knew the answer before the words came out of my mouth. I had to remember that people who are hurting often hurt others. Those who do not receive healthy love in their earlier years don't really know how to respond when genuine love is presented. You reach out to them, but because of where they are mentally, they distort that love to make it fit their hurting reality. I wrestled with that pain for a long time, but then one Sunday morning I heard the Spirit of the Lord speak to my heart. *Shirley, just let it go.*

That was my sermon that Sunday morning. "The Lord wants us to let the vile words people say about us just flow off our backs. That doesn't mean we should pick up a snake and put him in our bosom. After all, a snake is a snake. But we can drop that snake to the floor and let it slither away. We can love a person in spite of what they may say about us, because the Lord blesses you when you can return good for evil." Since that time, that person no longer attends our church. However, they visit periodically. I have accepted their apology, and I have forgiven them. But I simply will not allow a snake to bite me twice.

Over the years since Dr. King's death, we have come a little closer to realizing his dream, but we have a long way to go. Incidents such as the Rodney King beating in Los Angeles demonstrate the reality that America still struggles with racial tensions, suspicions, and mistrust. And regardless of what one may think about the guilt or innocence of O. J.

Simpson, the trial clearly shows that Americans still see things differently when it comes to matters of justice and law. The battle over affirmative action also illustrates the same kinds of issues.

Black Americans continue to struggle in our fight against racial prejudice. Things have improved to a large degree since the days of the early sixties, but by no means have we arrived. We are a strong people with a profound faith in God, and with God on our side we will continue to persevere to take our places as equal citizens in this great country. I believe it is imperative that we continue to push for political, social, and health care reform. We are all entitled to life, liberty, and the pursuit of happiness. But while we are reaching for freedom, we must realize that real freedom is only in Christ Jesus. That is why I am committed to singing and preaching the Word of God. Jesus proclaimed, "You shall know the truth, and the truth shall make you free"—free from prejudice and racism; free from hate, bitterness, and mistrust; free from poverty and despair. I am determined to keep singing, preaching, and teaching until I hear the bells of freedom ringing in our homes, in our cities, in our country, and in our nation. Then we can declare as Dr. Martin Luther King Jr. did, "Free at last! Free at last! Thank God Almighty, we are free at last!"

CHAPTER EIGHT

First Lady

THE MELODY

You are everything that we need;
through winter, summer, spring, or fall.
All of the countless times we've failed;
yet Your grace still prevails.
Lord, You're everything;
let the praises ring;
Lord, You're everything we need.
—"Everything We Need"

AND THE WORD

Who then is Paul, and who is Apollos,
but ministers through whom you believed,
as the Lord gave each one?
I planted, Apollos watered, but God gave the increase.
So then neither he who plants is anything, nor he who waters,
but God who gives the increase.
—1 Corinthians 3:5–7

—————— IN 1971, five years after leaving the Caravans, the National Academy of Recording Arts and Sciences, composed of my peers and executives of the music industry, conferred upon me the highest honor that any musician can receive. They voted me the winner of a Grammy Award, the Oscar of the music world. My recording "Put Your Hand in the Hand of the Man from Galilee" had won in the category of Best Soul Gospel Performance. To say the least, I was ecstatic. I could not believe that I had actually won a Grammy! Weeks earlier when word of my nomination had come, I never considered the possibility that there was the slightest chance of my receiving that coveted award. After all, the category was extremely competitive, and the other artists were, by far, better known nationally than I was. In fact, I was so certain that I would not win that I, for the most part, dismissed the nomination out of my mind and never entertained the thought of attending the award ceremonies. But I must admit, at the time I was humbled and surprised to learn that I had actually been recognized by the industry. Winning that Grammy took me completely by surprise.

On the night of the ceremony I was in concert in a little city called Houma, Louisiana, outside of New Orleans. We had been on tour most of that week, singing nightly in different cities. Enthused by the move of God that we were experiencing, I was completely engrossed in those services and oblivious to the Grammy Awards taking place far away in Los Angeles, California. To be honest, I had not thought about that event since the news of my nomination. In addition to not believing I could win, part of my indifference toward the Grammys was based upon the fact that I just didn't know how prestigious the awards were. Remember that this was over twenty-five years ago, and my knowledge of the business side of the music industry was somewhat limited.

At any rate, I went to bed that night without giving the Grammy Awards a second thought. I was exhausted and completely worn out from traveling and singing several consecutive nights, so after the concert, I caught a quick bite to eat, slipped into my pajamas, and climbed into bed. Within minutes I fell fast asleep. I doubt if a riot outside my hotel room could have awakened me that night.

Early the next morning, a hard knocking at the door disturbed my sleep. Not wanting to completely awaken, I yelled out from the bed, "Please go away."

The knocking continued. The person at the door was also yelling. I pulled a pillow over my head, but the person outside would not give up.

Finally, unable to ignore the knocking any longer, I emerged from under the pillow and immediately recognized the voice outside the door. It was my sister Anne. She was yelling at the top of her voice.

"Shirley Ann, get out of bed," she shouted. "I've got something to tell you."

"Tell me through the door," I groaned. "I'm too tired to get up."

"You won a Grammy!" she yelled. "I heard it on the news! You won a Grammy! Get up! You won a Grammy!"

About the third time she yelled it, I realized what she was saying. You'd better believe I jumped out of bed then, throwing the covers all over the floor. I put on a robe, ran across the room, and threw open the door. Anne and I started hugging and shouting and dancing, right there outside the hotel room. I am sure if anyone had seen us that morning, they would have thought we were crazy. It was one of the most exciting times in my life, a day I will never forget.

Later that week, I returned home, and my Grammy was delivered in the mail. I unwrapped it and placed it in the center of Mama's mantel. Everyone who entered our house could see that Baby Shirley Caesar had won a Grammy.

Unfortunately, I no longer have that Grammy. All the others I have subsequently won are sitting in a trophy case in my home, but my first Grammy is gone. It was stolen from me in a very subtle manner.

A Grammy is shaped like a gramophone, an old-fashioned record player, with a megaphone extending from its top, and it sits on a square bottom base.

A few months after winning it, I was dusting the mantel over our fireplace and accidentally knocked the Grammy to the floor, breaking off the megaphone piece. I had no idea where to get it repaired, so I placed it back on the mantel. A short time later, a lady, who claimed to have known my father when he was alive, came to visit me. I had never seen her before and cannot, to this day, remember her name. We talked at length, and I discovered that she knew things about my father and my family, which led me to believe she was who she said she was—an old friend of my family. I didn't see any reason to be suspicious of her, but I should have been.

When she saw the broken Grammy, she told me she knew someone who could repair it for me. I should have known better, but I allowed her to take it with her when she left, trusting her to have it repaired and to return it to me. I never saw her or my Grammy again. Maybe someday I will get it back, who knows? Thankfully, it wasn't the only Grammy I would receive. But I did have to wait almost a decade before winning another one.

After Mahalia Jackson died in 1972, many people began referring to me as the Queen of Gospel Music. I wasn't comfortable with that, and I tried to discourage that type of accolade because in my opinion no one but Mahalia Jackson would ever deserve that title, past, present, or future. I described myself then, and I describe myself now, as a traditional gospel singer with a contemporary flavor. In other words, I am just a down-to-earth singer serving an up-to-date God. If anyone other than Mahalia Jackson is deserving of the title Queen of Gospel, I think it should be Albertina Walker.

As my style of music evolved and I gained more experience, several wonderful opportunities came my way. In 1974 I was featured on two compilation albums with James Cleveland, the King of Gospel. Those albums, entitled *King and Queen of Gospel, Volume One,* and *King and Queen of Gospel, Volume Two,* added even more validity to the fact that God was certainly blessing my ministry. Singing on the same recording with such a great man was an undeniable honor.

The year 1975 was another monumental one for me. It was the year that I experienced my first national recording hit. The song "No Charge," which I recorded on the Hob Record label, became my first certified gold record. It crossed over the gospel lines and received a great deal of airplay on the country stations. A personal favorite of mine, this song tells the story of a mother and her son. One day the son comes to his mother with a list of the chores he does every day. Beside each chore, he has affixed a price he feels his mother should pay him for his labor. "For mowing the yard, $5.00; for making up my own bed, $1.00; for going to the store, $.50; for playing with little brother while you went shopping, $.25; for taking out the trash, $1.00; for getting a good report card, $5.00; and for raking the yard, $2.00. Total owed, $14.75."

The mother looks at the list her son had compiled and then looks at her son. While doing so, a thousand memories flash through her mind. She turns the paper over and writes these words: "For the nine months I carried you, growing inside me, no charge. For the nights I sat up with you, doctored you, and prayed for you, no charge. For the time and the tears, and the cost through the years, there is no charge, my son. When you add it all up, the full cost of my love is no charge."

I loved that song, and it appeared our listening audience loved it also, especially in the Caribbean Islands. In all of our concerts it was our most requested song. Even today, it is still a part of our concert repertoire.

From that point on, the Lord seems to have established me as a noted gospel singer. But popularity and recognition are always accompanied by some degree of danger. This can take the form of stalking, telephone harassment, or obscene mail. I've experienced them all. I particularly recall this mentally deranged man from Baton Rouge, Louisiana, who honestly thought he was my father and kept calling the police department in Durham trying to get in touch with me. When he couldn't get my unpublished telephone number from directory assistance, he called the police, telling them that he was my father and needed to contact me.

Following through on his request, the police called me at home one night and told me that my father had called them to get my number. I said to the officer, "Sir, my father is dead!"

The policeman said, "According to this gentleman, he is your father, he is in Baton Rouge, Louisiana, and he called us to find you."

I said, "That is not my father. My father has been dead since 1945."

The officer said, "I understand Ms. Caesar. We'll take care of it."

But this deranged man would not give up. Next he began calling my office, ranting and raging that he was my father and that I had better call him or else. It was not at all uncommon for me to call my office for messages, and one of my staff would jokingly tell me, "Your father called again, very agitated and very irate." Of course, I failed to see the humor in the situation. In fact, during the time of his callings, we were scheduled for a concert in Baton Rouge, Louisiana, and while I knew the Lord had His hand of protection over my life, I was a bit apprehensive about going. After all, we didn't know what this man looked like or what his real mental state was. He could be one of several hundred people in the audience and could try anything. As a result, the concert sponsors added additional security, and, thank God, the concert took place without incident.

Finally, hoping to put a stop to it, I decided to call the man. I tried to reason with him. "Sir," I said. "My father is dead. He died when I was a little girl."

"No," he insisted. "I'm your father. Your real name is White. The Caesars adopted you from me."

I asked him, "How old are you?"

He said, "Forty-six."

I almost laughed. "I'm older than you," I said. "How could you be my father?"

"I don't know," he said. "All I know is I'm your father."

I then knew, conclusively, he had a problem, and I hung the phone up. To this very day he continues to call my office, insisting he's my father.

Notoriety will often bring this type of individual into a life. And it will also bring various temptations and allurements that, if you are not careful, you will fall prey to. The key to avoiding these types of pitfalls is found in the Bible, James 4:7–8: "Therefore submit to God. Resist the devil and he will flee from you. Draw near to God and He will draw near to you." All of my life I have tried to walk according to

God's statutes and to do those things that are pleasing in His sight. I don't want my life to end up as a mockery of God.

I am very careful not to judge or make any assumptions about anyone. We have all made mistakes and have all failed God at some point or other, but that does not mean that we have not repented and received God's forgiveness. I have found that long after God has forgiven you, man will yet condemn you. But you should never look down on a person unless you are lending him a hand to pick him up. And never, never kick a person when he is down, because one day, you just may need a friend yourself.

Without question, notoriety has its advantages and disadvantages, its positives and negatives. Whatever recognition the Lord has allowed me to attain, I try to use it as a platform to present Jesus to the world. It is imperative that I stay focused and ever cognizant of what my purpose in life is. I am here to serve God and my fellow man. Long ago I adopted this philosophy for my life: "Christ first, others second, myself last." I have tried to exemplify this maxim in my everyday living.

The year before I received my first Grammy, in 1970, I implemented the Shirley Caesar Outreach Ministries, Inc., as the vehicle through which I have endeavored to provide food, clothing, shelter, and emergency funds to the underprivileged and needy. There is also a viable Christian outreach component consisting of radio broadcasting, revivals, crusades, and gospel concerts. Our primary purpose is to minister to the total man, which includes both his physical and spiritual welfare. It is my contention that there is no better way of serving God than through serving my fellow man.

I'll never forget the day the Lord placed in my spirit the overwhelming desire to somehow assist in feeding the hungry of the world.

My group and I were performing in Miami during the Thanksgiving holidays. And while we were there, the Consolers, Sullivan and Iola Pugh, a husband-and-wife gospel team, invited us, along with several other groups who were also in the area, to their home for Thanksgiving dinner. We were all enjoying the fellowship and eagerly awaiting the scrumptious meal being prepared in the kitchen. Even the aroma was delicious. Most of the men had gathered around the television to watch the football game. Around 6:00, Sis Pugh called out, "Dinner is ready!" Because there were so many of us, the meal was served buffet style. A young lady assisting with the serving of the meal said to me, "Evangelist Caesar, what part of the turkey do you prefer?"

I said, "I want the turkey wing. I love wings."

She prepared my plate with a turkey wing, dressing, vegetables, and all the other trimmings, and I sat in the living room with the TV tray in front of me. We all bowed our heads, thanking God for the meal we were about to receive. I was about to eat when I noticed a documentary was being shown on television. Its subject disturbed me intensely. The documentary was portraying the starving, emaciated children in the world. There were awful images of thin, potbellied, crying children in Ethiopia, Bangladesh, Somalia, and other parts of Africa and Asia. Surprisingly, however, the primary focus was on children starving not just in these Third World countries but right here in the United States, even as close as my neighboring state, Tennessee. I was troubled by what I saw. Here I was about to feast on a delectable meal, and there were children without even so much as a morsel of bread to eat.

I was about to take my first bite of food when I heard the Lord speak to my spirit. *Shirley, feed My sheep.*

Thinking this had a spiritual implication, I responded,

"But, Lord, I'm already doing that. I'm singing and preaching continuously. I'm sharing Your Word everywhere I go. I'm feeding Your sheep with the gospel of Jesus Christ."

Still I heard the same words repeatedly in my spirit. *Feed My sheep. Feed My sheep.*

Again I replied, "Lord, I am already doing that."

The Lord spoke to me the third time, the same as when He questioned the apostle Peter: "Loveth thou Me?" After Peter had answered in the affirmative three times, the Lord responded, *Feed My sheep.*

By then I felt completely bewildered and perplexed. When I returned home, I did what I always do when I am confused about something—I talked to Mama. When I told her what the Lord had said, she asked me, "What were you doing when the Lord spoke to you?"

"I was about to eat Thanksgiving dinner, and I was watching a documentary on world hunger."

Mama said, "Shirley, it's simple. The Lord wasn't talking about spiritual food. He was talking about natural food."

Leave it to my mother to unravel the mystery and make it so plain. Of course, that's what the Lord meant.

Knowing God's will, I began working diligently to obey Him. I established the Shirley Caesar Outreach Ministries, and before Christmas we had raised enough funds and collected enough food to provide food baskets to over five hundred families. Since then, the ministry has expanded beyond just feeding the hungry.

Today we provide a vast array of community support. We conduct seminars on a wide range of topics such as AIDS prevention, teenage pregnancy prevention, alcohol recovery, educational assistance, and family relationships. On a daily basis, we try to feed the hungry and provide shelter for the homeless and financial support for people needing help with rent, utility bills, and clothing. We provide fans for the elderly during the hot summers and heaters and blankets during the cold winters. We know we can't do all things for all people, but we can do some things for some people. Symbolically, I can't sweeten the entire Atlantic Ocean with one cup of sugar, but I can certainly take a pitcherful out and sweeten it.

My ministry would be one-sided and unbalanced if all I ever did was sing and preach about giving and sharing and caring for the less fortunate, and not actively involve myself in doing just that. We are called to be not just hearers of the Word but also doers of the Word. As Jesus said, "Inasmuch as you did it to one of the least of these My brethren, you did it to Me." When we serve our fellow man we are, in effect, serving Christ.

Not only did I achieve my first gold record with "No Charge" in 1975, but also that year *Ebony* magazine presented me with their Ebony Award for Best Female Gospel Singer. In many ways that award meant more to me than my Grammy Award. It meant that my people, the African-American community, viewed me as a positive role model and a respected representative of my race, and for that I was very thankful. Even today, I treasure that award.

The year 1975 proved to be a very pivotal one for me. It was the year my recording contract with Hob Records ended, and I opted not to re-sign. By my own election, it was almost two years before I finally consented to sign with another label. I needed time to reflect and reevaluate my sense of direction. My primary purpose as a Christian and as a gospel singer has always been to reach as many people as possible with the message of Jesus, regardless of race, gender, demographic location, or socioeconomic status. At Hob Records I didn't feel that purpose was being adequately accomplished. The company that could help me achieve that objective was the next one I wanted to sign with. I thought I had found that company in Roadshow Records. As it turned out I was wrong.

I signed with Roadshow Records in 1977. Although this company was smaller than Hob Records, its president, Fred Frank, and its producer, Michael Stokes, had, as they phrased it, big, big plans. They brought me into their office to tell me what they had in mind.

"We want you to do a more contemporary gospel," said Frank. "We want to break your music out into a broader market."

"Yeah, like Andrae Crouch and the Disciples," said Stokes. "We think you've got what it takes to do that, and Roadshow is the company to help you do it."

"We're ready to put our best promotion behind you and make you more successful than you ever dreamed," Frank added.

"We want you to stay true to your gospel roots," said Stokes. "Just make it more modern, more sophisticated."

"You will be the first woman with Roadshow Records," said Frank. "Together, we can take you to the top."

That sounded attractive to me. Stay true to my roots, but move into a broader spectrum and increase my audience outreach. I recorded my first album with Roadshow, and they called it *First Lady*. People in the music industry misinterpreted this title and thought we were trying to make a statement about my status in the music world, but we really weren't. I was simply the first lady to ever record on their label. At any rate, the title caught on, and newspapers, magazines, and music executives began referring to me as the "First Lady of Gospel."

While at Roadshow I learned a valuable lesson. Innovative marketing strategies and extensive advertising campaigns are no guarantee that you will expand your market share, particularly if the market you are trying to penetrate is not ready for what you are trying to present. In spite of our best efforts, my first album with Roadshow did not do nearly as well as we had hoped. In retrospect, I now clearly understand why. Roadshow had tried to present me as a more contemporary gospel artist, because they thought that would attract a broader market segment. But the gospel music world was not quite ready to receive that from me. They didn't know what to make of that *First Lady* album. All of my life I had sung only traditional gospel, and then all of a sudden I came out with a contemporary gospel sound. My listening audience didn't respond to it at all. To say the least, I endured a great deal of criticism because of the recording. And to be very honest, I was very uncomfortable recording that album. When I voiced my concerns to Roadshow executives, I was told, in so many words, that I really didn't have a choice in the matter.

The *First Lady* album had horns, electric guitars, keyboards, and drums. You name it and we used it. In actuality, among other things, the album was overproduced. Only two songs on the album were received favorably, "Faded Rose" and "Miracle Worker," the two songs that I brought to the recording session. In fact, "Faded Rose" became quite popular and is still played by radio announcers across the country, particularly around the celebration of Mother's Day. It reflected my true traditional style of singing and demonstrated what was readily becoming my song-sermon trademark.

"Faded Rose" relates the story of a young man who grew up and moved from the United States to Germany. While there he was critically wounded and placed in a medical facility. Unknown to him, his mother dies. His family tried to find him in time for him to be able to attend his mother's funeral, but to no avail. Upon being released from the hospital, the young man finds out about his mother's death and rushes home. The next time we see him he's in leg braces, standing over his mother's grave, with one faded red rose in his hand, and this is what he says:

> *Petals from this faded rose is all I have to give,*
> *But, Mama, I tried to make you happy while you lived.*
> *If I had a million dollars, I'd line your grave with gold.*
> *But that wouldn't wake you from your sleep*
> *as eternal ages roll.*
> *So petals from this faded rose is all I have to give,*
> *But, Mama, I tried to make you happy while you lived.*

People responded well to that song, just as they had responded to "No Charge." It reminded them that relationships are very important, particularly children's relationships with their parents. "Faded Rose" was a wake-up call to all of us that if we love and appreciate someone, it is very important to tell them and show them while they are alive and with us, because after they are gone, it is too late.

After *First Lady*, I recorded only one more album with Roadshow Records: *Shirley Caesar, From the Heart*. While a few songs on it echoed my favored traditional style, others had too much of a contemporary flair. The acceptance and sales of that recording, just as with *First Lady*, were mediocre.

Throughout the remainder of the seventies, I continued to perform in concerts, preach in churches, and take care of my mother. As I did so, a number of wonderful opportunities to be a witness for Christ came my way. In 1976 I traveled to Germany, singing for the soldiers in the armed forces. Although it was difficult, being a young lady all alone in a foreign country where very little English is spoken, the experience was quite educational and incited within me a renewed appreciation for the United States. Without a doubt, we are a blessed nation.

In 1978 I received my first opportunity to sing the "Star Spangled Banner" for the opening of a New York Knicks basketball game at Madison Square Garden and for a New York Giants football game at Shea Stadium. That same year I appeared as the guest artist for the Congressional Black Caucus in Washington, D.C., and I sang at the tenth anniversary of the Dove Awards held at Opryland in Nashville, Tennessee.

Although I was no longer recording with Roadshow Records, I was determined to continue using the gift of song the Lord had blessed me with for the upbuilding of His kingdom. Yes, I was without a recording contract, but by no means was I depressed or disappointed, because I knew that everything moved according to God's timing and that nothing was predicated upon man's decision. My life and career were totally in God's hands. I was completely dependent upon Him, and the absence of a recording contract would not cause me to doubt Him. Through every adversity, I always take the stance that Job took, "Though He slay me, yet will I trust Him." An illness I had during this time reminded me of just how helpless we are without the Lord.

We had just arrived in Philadelphia for a concert performance the following night. After checking into the hotel we all decided to retire early so that we would be at our best for the next evening's performance. I felt fine prior to going to bed, a little tired from traveling, but nothing out of the ordinary. The next morning I woke up in excruciating pain and could barely move. Instantly I knew I was in trouble and needed help. I knew I was in too much pain to get to the telephone, which was on the other side of the room. But my sister Anne's room was next door, and somehow I managed to fall slowly out of bed and began banging on the wall behind the bed, trying to get her attention.

Anne finally heard my banging and came running to my room. But I couldn't get to the door to let her in, so she called security. Finding me on the floor doubled over in pain, she immediately said, "I'm taking you to the doctor." We were scheduled to sing that evening, so we called the concert promoter to let him know what was happening. He said, "Before you go to the doctor, let me send my pastor over."

The pastor arrived, along with another minister. They prayed for me, but the pain persisted. (That is not to say that God is not a healer, because He is. For even when man operates, God has to heal.)

Around 2:00 P.M., the pain was so severe that Anne took me to the emergency room at City Line Hospital.

While examining me, the doctor touched the lower right side of my back, and the pain was so intense that I literally jumped off the table.

He immediately knew what was wrong. "You have kidney stones. As soon as you get home, you need to make an appointment to see a urologist."

Through the grace of God, the pain subsided enough for me to perform the concert that night. But during the course of the next few days the pain kept increasingly getting worse. I had no choice. I finally went to Duke University Medical Center in Durham.

There the doctors ran extensive tests and took numerous X rays. Sure enough, when the diagnosis came in, it confirmed what the emergency room doctor in Philadelphia had previously told me—I had kidney stones. The prognosis was that I needed to have my right kidney removed. As they put it,

"The inside of that kidney is badly damaged from the stones and needs to come out."

The next morning the doctors came to my room with the consent papers for me to sign for the operation. For a few minutes, I just stared at the papers, thinking things over. Then I told the doctors, "Before I sign any papers, I want to get a second opinion."

They said, "Fine. We'll get another doctor to drop in and check you out."

I shook my head. "No," I said, "I don't want you to send anyone else. I've got another Doctor who makes house calls, and He's in my family."

One of the doctors said, "I know all of your mother's children, and you don't have any doctors in your family. You couldn't be talking about your brother Julius."

I said, "No, I'm talking about Jesus."

They looked at me as if I was crazy.

"Just let me go home for the night. I'll come back in the morning with these papers signed if that's what *my Doctor* tells me to do."

They shrugged and said okay. I checked out of the hospital in terrible pain. I felt sick, sick, sick. With the help of some of my family, I made it home and got dressed for bed. My sister turned down the covers of my bed and told me to get in. I said, "Wait a minute. Before I get in, I've got to go down." I fell to my knees.

The pain cut into my side. The gown I was wearing felt like a hot burning cloth. With my face buried in the covers and my spirit looking up to the Lord, I began to pray. "Lord, You know I have been traveling around the country in and out of every city imaginable, telling everyone that You're a healer. I know You can heal me. I have trusted You this far, so I'm giving this situation completely to You."

Almost immediately, a sense of contentment overshadowed me, and I heard the Lord speak. *Rest in Me, rest in Me.* That was enough for me.

I told the Lord, "All right, you have said it, and I am going to do just that. I can't preach one thing and then do something else. If I preach it, I have to exemplify it. You said to rest in you, so that's what I'm going to do."

The next morning, I went back to Duke Medical Center, still hurting in my side. I handed the envelope containing the papers to the doctor.

He opened the envelope and stared down at the papers. "You didn't sign them," he said.

"Nope," I said, "I didn't. I'm resting in the Lord."

He just shook his head. My faith said everything would be all right.

I requested another set of X rays to be taken of my kidney. Just as they were completed, the pain suddenly left. I jumped off the table and put on my clothes. Dr. Johnson, one of the best-known physicians in the nation, studied the new X rays for a moment and then handed them to the technician. The two of them left the room. A few minutes later, they returned, scratching their heads. They couldn't find anything wrong with my kidney!

They looked at me like the cat that had swallowed the canary. I pointed my finger at the doctor. "Didn't I tell you that God would heal me?" I said. "Didn't I tell you?"

I know emphatically that the Lord healed me. From that day to this, the pain has never returned. The Lord gave me a brand new kidney. The doctor's X ray revealed a perfectly normal, undamaged kidney. Make no mistake about it, the Lord is the Master Physician. He is always available, and we never have to make an appointment. We can come boldly to the throne of grace and ask for His help in the time of need.

Just as those kidney stones miraculously disappeared, before I knew it the seventies had also disappeared. A new decade began, and with it my ministry continued to grow and my opportunities to witness for the Lord continued to expand. But something else, something very wonderful, also happened in my personal life during the eighties. In 1983 I got married.

CHAPTER NINE

Wait on the Lord

########## THE MELODY ##########

I'm going to wait on the Lord
My blessings are on the way
I'm going to wait on the Lord
No matter what the people say

He said He would put no more on me
than I'd be able to bear
And whenever I need a friend I can call Him
and He'll be right there.
If I delight myself in Him
He will give me the desires of my heart
I won't worry, or complain or fret or cry
I'll let God do His job
I'm going to wait on the Lord
My deliverance is on the way
I'm going to wait on the Lord
My healing is on the way
When I don't know what to do
He steps right in and brings me through
When I have tried and tried and failed

127

that's when the Lord's grace prevails
I'm going to wait on the Lord
Waiting . . . with all of my heart
Waiting . . . sometimes the road is long
Waiting . . . but I refuse to give up on the Lord
I'm going to wait on the Lord
—"Wait on the Lord"

AND THE WORD

Love suffers long and is kind;
love does not envy;
love does not parade itself, is not puffed up;
does not behave rudely, does not seek its own,
is not provoked, thinks no evil;
does not rejoice in iniquity, but rejoices in the truth;
bears all things, believes all things,
hopes all things, endures all things.
Love never fails.
—1 Corinthians 13:4–8

——— OFTEN people ask me why I waited so long to marry. In our society it is expected that you marry somewhere between the ages of twenty and thirty. And although the individual pursuit of career goals has caused this age expectancy to rise over the last decade, it is still expected that most people will definitely marry before the age of forty.

Before I married in 1983 I faced a great deal of teasing because of my single status. Friends and family members would jokingly tell me that I was too particular and would never find anyone to meet my standards. Or they would say that if I didn't marry soon that after a while I would be too old and no one would want me. Of course, their taunting didn't bother me because I knew, as I knew with all other facets of my life, that the Lord had this area in control also. Meeting the person with whom I would spend the rest of my life would happen according to God's timing.

Like any single young lady I desired to have the American Dream, a husband, children, and a nice home, but I wanted a mate who would understand and support my call to the ministry. Consequently, I was determined that when I married it would be to someone who shared my love for the Lord, someone who wouldn't object to my taking care of my mother, someone who loved me, and someone whom I loved. Under no circumstances would I allow myself to be pressured into marrying someone simply because I was getting older.

During my twenties and thirties, as I sang with the Caravans and later with my own group, the Shirley Caesar Singers, I had the opportunity to meet several eligible Christian bachelors. And during that period, I received more marriage proposals than I can remember. It seems that almost every month someone was asking my mother for my hand in marriage. But to be very honest, I was so preoccupied with my ministry and career that I just didn't have the time to cultivate a relationship. There wasn't any time to think about a serious commitment. Serving the Lord and taking care of my mother took precedence in my life. At that time, marriage simply wasn't a priority.

Of course, I didn't take many of those proposals very seriously. I don't know how many I received because of my unquestioned beauty and charming personality. (Just kidding.) But I am sure that many came not because of who I really am but because of who some men perceived me to be. And that is a personality with some celebrity status, possibly a little economic security, and, in short, a good catch.

While there were those who were very assertive in seeking my hand in marriage, there were others who were very uncomfortable and insecure in my presence. Again, because they perceived me as a "celebrity," they found it difficult to just relax and be themselves. Regrettably they found it necessary to put on a facade to appear to be something or someone they were not, or they would try to demean me in an effort to project an air of superiority.

When I finally met the man who later became my husband, it happened quite unexpectedly. Harold Ivory Williams was the senior bishop of the Mount Calvary Holy Churches of America, the same denomination in which I grew up and was yet a member. Consequently, I knew of him and he knew of me long before we actually met. From a spiritual standpoint we had a great deal in common. We possessed the same religious convictions, held the same biblical tenets, and were both ministers of the gospel. Most important, he had a desire to serve the Lord that equaled mine. From a natural standpoint, Bishop Williams (as he is affectionately known) had many other positive qualities that I admired in a man, namely warmth, stability, generosity, humor, and strength. He was confident of himself and had a keen sense of self-worth. I knew he would not be intimidated by any measure of success I might ultimately attain.

I met Bishop Williams in January of 1983 during the citywide revival held annually in Durham. The Ministerial Alliance of our city had invited him to be the guest minister, and I sang during the opening service. The next day he invited me to lunch, and the rest is history. Two weeks later he proposed over the telephone. I turned him down the first time he asked. In fact, I turned him down the next time and the next and the next. After four proposals over the telephone, I told him, "If you are serious about marrying me, come to Durham and

ask." A week later he arrived from Baltimore with an engagement ring in the shape of the number nine and outlined with
nine diamonds. The diamonds represented the nine gifts of
the Holy Spirit. He took me to dinner that night and, while
there, again proposed. This time I knew I would say yes and
mean it with all of my heart and a piece of my liver. (Smile.)
I turned to Bishop Williams and said, "Yes, I will marry you,
but there is one stipulation. There is one thing you need to
know."

He reached over and took me by the hand. "What is
that?"

"I have been taking care of my mother since I was twelve
years old, and I will continue to care for her the rest of her
life." I then asked him, "Will that be a problem for you?"

He smiled, and I felt a warm sense of security encircle
me.

"I'm glad you brought this up," he said with a calm voice.
"I want you to know something also."

"What is it?" I asked.

"Not only will I not keep you from caring for your mother,
but I will help you take care of her," he said.

He had given the right answer. I began to smile as I replied,
"Then you have yourself a bride."

"And a mother," he added.

After five proposals I had said yes. Bishop Williams's per-
sistence and perseverance had won me over. If he was that
determined to marry me, perhaps he would be that determined to keep me.

The next day he went to see my mother. He walked into
her bedroom where she was sitting and knelt down beside
her big chair. When he asked her for my hand in marriage,
she told him he was the third bishop who had asked her
permission to marry me. But she must have recognized

something special in Bishop Williams because she immediately said yes.

Five months later, we were married in an incredible ceremony held at the Durham High School Auditorium. This was the largest wedding ever in the city of Durham. We did not intend for it to become so enormous, but things just seemed to get out of control before we knew it. Everyone wanted to be a part of the wedding party.

Our wedding took place on June 26, 1983. Over four thousand family members, friends, and well-wishers were present. Our wedding party included three best men, two maids of honor, one matron of honor, twenty-three bridesmaids and groomsmen, fourteen junior bridesmaids and junior groomsmen, and an assembly of flower girls, trainbearers, and candle bearers. Three different ministers officiated. A total of one hundred and six people were in our wedding party. Of course everyone present could not get into the auditorium, so they crowded the streets outside, which police escorts had blocked off.

The day was extremely hot, and the Durham High School Auditorium was not equipped with an air-conditioning system. It felt like a sauna inside of that building. Someone later joked that because of the stifling heat, three ministers were definitely needed—one to hold me up, one to hold Bishop Williams up, and one to administer the vows. It took an hour and a half for the entire wedding party to march down the aisle. Bishop Williams and I sang to each other. He sang "You Are So Beautiful to Me," and I sang a medley of songs to him, which included, "Let It Be Me," and "We Can Make It Together." Not only did we both sing, but also George Scott, one of the original Five Blind Boys, added his voice to the festivities. He had been such a good friend over the years that I wanted him to be a part of my special day. My sister Anne and the Shirley Caesar Singers sang "I'll Be There." Would you believe that she was trying to shout the audience on that song? My nephew Gerald Caesar sang "Cabin in the Sky," and my niece Tammy actually brought the house down as she sang the Lord's Prayer. The wedding lasted three hours.

When the ceremony ended, Bishop Williams and I rode off in a horse-drawn carriage. Our reception was held at the Durham Civic Center. The wedding cake stood over five feet tall. Someone remarked that it was just a little taller than I was. For our honeymoon we spent one week in Hawaii and another in London. I didn't intend for my wedding to be so extravagant, but I have no regrets that it was. After all, I only planned to do it once.

Much of society's problems today evolve from the dissolution of the family unit. When marriages fail, children are usually the casualties. They are the ones who suffer the most, and suffering children generally resort to deviant behavior. That is why it is imperative that those contemplating marriage realize that they are about to enter into a lifelong commitment, one that must be built upon a solid foundation if their marriage is to survive. Without the proper preparation for marriage, when problems arise, and they will, the husband and wife will find themselves seeking a divorce instead of seeking a remedy and staying together.

I strongly recommend that before a couple marry they seek counsel from their minister, a marriage counselor, or their parents. As a minister of the gospel, a personal requirement of mine is that, before I consent to perform the wedding ceremony for any couple pondering marriage, they must first schedule a counseling session with me, preferably before the wedding date is set.

I believe that in order for a marriage to be successful, there are certain aspects that must be discussed and considered beforehand. There are basically twelve points I propose to those with whom I counsel.

1. *Marry someone with whom you have things in common.* The common thread in every marriage should be Jesus Christ. Christians should marry Christians. The Scriptures remind us not to be unequally yoked.

Believers who marry nonbelievers will definitely experience conflicts of interest in their relationship. The two lifestyles are usually largely incompatible. Of course Christian spouses are just as susceptible to mistakes as everyone else, but they are keenly aware of the sanctity of marriage and know the true meaning of forgiveness and, therefore, will put more energy into saving a troubled marriage.

2. *Be sure you know the "real" person and not just the personality.* In other words, don't be fooled by the pretty wrapping paper on the box. Make sure you know what is inside of the box. A human body is nothing but a house, and you need to know who is living inside of it. Look further than the physical appearance of a person, because looks will not always last. They are temporal. But traits such as loyalty, honesty, compassion, and consideration will continue long after physical beauty has faded. Take time to know each other. Spend quality time talking, and not just gazing into each other's eyes. Discover each other's likes, dislikes, dreams, and aspirations. You should know how they react under pressure and stress. Observe how they behave when angry. I have counseled couples who knew absolutely nothing about their future mate, not even their favorite color. During the period of courtship everyone projects their best image. It is imperative that you know both sides of your future mate. After the honeymoon there should not be any surprises.

3. *Don't marry someone thinking you can change them.* Honey, you don't have that kind of power. If he is an alcoholic

when you marry him, he will be one afterward. If he is a womanizer before you marry him, a ring on his finger will not stop him from cheating on you. If he is lazy and irresponsible while you are dating him, he will be lazy and irresponsible after you marry him.

Now, of course, the Lord can change anyone, regardless of their adverse habits. But I would suggest that you allow the transformation to take place before you consent to be their spouse. Your love may be strong, but your love is not strong enough to change anyone.

4. *Save yourself sexually for the mate God has for you.* In a world that condones and promotes premarital sex, I know it is very difficult to remain pure. The motto of the world is "If it feels good, go for it." But you must realize that these are the days of AIDS and other sexually transmitted diseases that can and will kill you. In the hair salon I patronize, a jar of contraceptives sits on the counter for the convenience of anyone who may want or need them, regardless of age. But contraceptives are no guarantee for safe sex. You place yourself in a high-risk category when you are involved sexually with more than one partner. Ladies, men generally feel, "Why buy the cow, when the milk is free." Men, ladies tend to believe that men who are womanizers are "endangered species," and if they become involved with you, you place them at risk also. God intended for sex to be shared between two individuals only within the sanctity of marriage. Save yourself for the spouse that God has for you.

5. *Ladies, beware of the man who promises you the world to lure you into his bed.* If he is really sincere about giving you the world, the first thing he should want to give you is his last name. If you have to sleep with him to be the recipient of his promises, you can be sure he has made the same

promises to someone else. Ladies, if you go to bed with dogs, you will get up with fleas.

6. *When you begin thinking seriously about marrying someone, make a counseling appointment with your minister immediately, and definitely make an appointment before you set the wedding date.* As I have stated previously, I require this of every couple I marry, but too often we do just the opposite. We decide to get married, and then we seek counseling from our minister. But why then? You have already predetermined that you know what is best for you. In all likelihood, nothing the minister can say or do will change your decision. At that point you don't want to hear him discuss issues of compatibility, mutual interests, and potential problem areas. You definitely don't want to hear any suggestions of possibly canceling your wedding plans. After all, you are in love. Bear in mind that your minister is only trying to ensure that the person you have selected for your lifetime mate is the right person for you. A canceled wedding now is much better than a divorce three years later. Seek counseling before you make your final decision.

7. *Know something about the role expected of you in the marriage.* As a child I complained when my mother assigned housework to me. I didn't particularly like cleaning or cooking. When I complained about it, my mother always said, "I'm preparing you for your husband." Likewise, she would tell my brothers, "I'm preparing you for your wife."

I didn't know what she meant at the time, but I do now. Wives and husbands should know something about cooking, cleaning, budgeting, and running a household in general. In marriage, helping each other comes with the territory. There should be no stereotypes, particularly if both parties are working.

When I first began dating my husband, I didn't know how

to cook very well. I invited him over for dinner, but because of my limited culinary skills, I had a friend of mine prepare the meal. I didn't want him to know that I couldn't cook. I told him about it later, of course, but if I had paid closer attention to my mother in the kitchen, I would have been prepared for that experience.

8. *Realize that marriage is more than candlelight and roses.* Romance is a necessary ingredient in every marriage, and you should work hard at keeping it alive in your relationship. But romance alone will not keep the wheels of a marriage moving forward. After the honeymoon the real world sets in. Marriage is giving, sharing, and helping each other. Marriage is continuing to love your mate in spite of morning breath, uncombed hair, and an unshaven face. Marriage is cleaning the house, cooking dinner, cutting the grass, and repairing the car. Keeping the romance in your relationship entails sharing in all aspects of the marriage.

9. *A family that prays together, stays together.* There should be time allocated for daily family devotion. A husband and a wife should pray together and read the Bible together. You should attend worship service and weekly Bible study together. Be active in your church. Don't just send your children to Sunday school; take them. Keep Christ as the nucleus of your family. Statistics show that families who pray, study the Bible, and attend worship service experience less abuse, less poverty, and less divorce. Prayer will keep a marriage strong, and your children will be nurtured in a home where two people love each other and love the Lord.

10. *Never go to sleep angry with one another.* This is what the Bible teaches, and we should try to apply this principle in the marriage relationship. Learn how to say "I'm sorry." It doesn't matter if you feel you were not at fault. Every husband and wife should practice forgiveness. Bishop

Williams and I work hard at this. It is not always easy, because like every married couple we have our disputes and disagreements, and each of us, at times, have felt that we were right. But then we realize that it is not about who is right or wrong; it is about two people who love each other and are willing to forgive and forget.

11. Learn to give constructive criticism without attacking each other. Communication is the key to any relationship, especially marriage. But destructive communication can hurt more than no communication. In other words, persistent criticism of your mate will certainly damage your marriage relationship. There are times when problems must be discussed, but it should not be done in a way that destroys the other person.

Criticism should always be done constructively and complemented with something positive. Practice accentuating the positive and suppressing the negative.

12. Find time to do things together. Find activities that you both enjoy, and spend quality time together. In today's society, husbands and wives are so busy with their jobs and the household duties that they hardly have time for each other. There should be a special time and a special place reserved just for you and your spouse. If a weekly time is not feasible, then a romantic getaway should be scheduled monthly. My husband and I travel together. We listen to gospel music together. We even enjoy solving crossword puzzles and playing Scrabble together. We both love the Lord with all our hearts, and, of course, we attend church together. We have a great deal in common.

At the time of this writing, Bishop Williams and I have been married fourteen years. We have faced many of the same challenges as other couples, but we have endured and have remained very much in love.

When my mother passed, I lapsed into a deep depression.

I was very sad and discouraged. I totally shut down. My mother had been my life. I did not want to go on without her. I hated getting up in the morning and facing the day without her. I didn't want to do anything but stare at the four walls in my bedroom. I thought about my mother constantly. I missed the times when I would go to her house and we would just sit around in her bedroom or in the kitchen laughing and talking. After she passed, I sometimes found myself going to her house, entering her bedroom, touching her chair, envisioning her sitting there.

The grief I experienced was immeasurable. My husband, realizing the pain I felt, did something I will never forget. One day he came into our bedroom and took me by the hand. "Come with me," he said. "Let's go for a walk."

"It's too cold outside, I don't want to go," I protested. We had just had an icy rain, and sleet was everywhere. But Bishop Williams insisted. Too weak from grief to resist, I put on a coat, boots, and a scarf and followed him out of the house. He led me through the neighborhood.

"Let's quote Scriptures," he said, squeezing my hand. "Victory Scriptures."

"I don't want to," I replied. I just wanted to cry, cry, cry. But he was persistent.

He began, "This too shall pass."

Crying and complaining I said, "I can do all things through Christ who strengthens me."

"Yea though I walk through the valley of the shadow of death, I will fear no evil . . . thy rod and thy staff, they comfort me," he quoted.

"I will lift up my eyes unto the hills—from whence comes my help? My help comes from the LORD," I continued.

"Weeping may endure for a night, but joy comes in the morning," he said.

We quoted Scripture after Scripture as we walked through the neighborhood. I guess the neighbors thought we were crazy. It was freezing cold outside and ice was literally bouncing off of our coats, but Bishop Williams and his grieving wife were walking through the community quoting Scriptures.

The more I recited the Word, the lighter my burden became. The more I reiterated them, the more I could feel the Lord strengthening me. By the time we completed our walk, I had "Scriptured" myself out of much of my grief. I have felt sadness since that day, but nothing comparable to what I was experiencing beforehand. My husband reminded me that there is deliverance from every situation in the Word of God. I love many things about my husband, but what I love the most is that he is a man of compassion who has totally dedicated himself to the work of the Lord. I have no regrets about waiting so long to get married. I waited on the Lord, and He blessed me with a wonderful husband. I have no doubts that Bishop Williams is the person the Lord intended for me to marry.

CHAPTER TEN

Returning to My Roots

THE MELODY

Speak a word into my spirit Lord,
I need to hear from you
My very soul is thirsty Lord
Just a word from You will do
Lord You are more than life to me
That's why I'm clinging close to Thee
I want to know You when You speak
It's Your face Lord I will seek
Send Your word Lord, send Your word Lord, In my spirit
If You speak into my spirit Lord
I know that I won't go wrong
If You send down Your word Lord
You'll give me strength to carry on
Give me ears to hear Your voice
In my life You are my choice
I want to know You when You speak
It's Your face Lord I will seek
Send Your word, send Your word, in my spirit
—"Just a Word"

⋯⋯⋯⋯⋯⋯⋯AND THE WORD⋯⋯⋯⋯⋯⋯⋯⋯⋯

And let us not grow weary while doing good,
for in due season we shall reap
if we do not lose heart.
—Galatians 6:9

———— BY the time I married in 1983, the Lord had
blessed my ministry enormously, and my career had taken
off in entirely new directions to unprecedented heights.
Successes were occurring at a level I could only have dreamed
of years before.

It seems to have all begun when I signed with Word Records
in 1980. My experience with Roadshow had convinced me
that it was time to consider making a change.

As I sought the Lord in prayer concerning the direction
I should take, I felt impressed in my spirit to sign with Word
Records. They were an all-gospel label, therefore, I was confident that they would not try to persuade me to sing about
Jesus in the second or third person. By that, I mean I could
freely use the name of Jesus and not have to refer to Him as
He or *You*. I have never wanted to do that and find it dis-
tasteful when others do. As gospel singers, we should not try
to camouflage who we are singing about. If we are taking a
stand for the Lord, then we should be emphatic about it.

After signing with Word Records, I began to record albums
in quick succession. In 1980 we released *Rejoice*, in 1981
Go, and in 1982 *Jesus, I Love Calling Your Name*. Afterward,
I took a much needed break for a year.

I was pleased with the results of those first three albums.
They did well. *Rejoice* won my second Grammy for Best Soul

Gospel Performance by a Female and the first of my Dove Awards for Inspirational Black Gospel Album of the Year.

Go produced my second Dove Award, this one for the Traditional Black Gospel Album of the Year. And although it didn't win any awards, *Jesus, I Love Calling Your Name* sold more copies than any of the others.

With the release of each of those albums, I found myself on the road even more. Pastors, promoters, and organizations from all around the country were constantly calling me and the Caesar Singers to come either for concerts or revivals. We were performing in excess of one hundred and fifty concerts per year. Between the release of the first two albums and the third, I got married. I was completely absorbed in my ministry and my new marital status, but that was nothing compared to what would happen next.

In 1984 I recorded my fourth album with Word, titled *Sailin' on the Sea of God's Love.* To my great surprise, it earned two Grammy Awards, one for Best Soul Gospel Performance by a Female and one for Best Soul Gospel Performance by a Duo for the title cut "Sailin' on the Sea of God's Love," which I recorded with Al Green. Additionally, it won a Dove Award, for Best Traditional Black Gospel Album.

As appreciative as I was of those awards, there were two others that I received in 1985 that meant even more to me: the NAACP Image Award and the *Essence* magazine award. Like the *Ebony* magazine award earlier, these also represented that the African-American community recognized my work in the field of gospel music and in the area of ministry. Each of these awards paid tribute to the fact that I had stayed close to my gospel roots, fulfilling the ministry that God had entrusted to me. I was deeply moved.

I will particularly forever remember the presentation of

the *Essence* award. Others honored that day included Maya Angelou, Winnie Mandela, Catherine Dunham, and Whitney Houston. Bill Cosby was the host. The ceremony was held at Radio City Music Hall in New York City. I recall the auditorium being filled with celebrities dressed in their after-five attire. The decorations were beautiful; flowers were everywhere. I felt so humbled that anyone would consider me worthy of such accolades. At that moment Proverbs 18:16 became alive in my heart—"A man's gift makes room for him, / And brings him before great men." Here I was sitting among all of these famous people.

The greatest honor came when Bill Cosby presented my award. I will never forget his words. Just before handing it to me, he said, "One of the things we know about Shirley Caesar is that she began in the church and she has remained in the church. Many other celebrities began their careers in the church and then wandered away from it. But not her. She is still where she is supposed to be—in the church."

I was flabbergasted to hear Bill Cosby say these words, because I never thought that he knew I existed. Thank you, Bill.

By the mid-eighties, the Lord had blessed my career even more. In 1985 and 1986 I recorded two more albums with Word Records, *Celebration* and *Christmasing,* both of which won additional awards. *Christmasing* won my fourth Dove Award for Best Traditional Black Gospel Album. The song "Martin" from *Celebration* won my fifth Grammy for Best Soul Gospel Performance by a Female.

Even though I was winning Grammy Awards and Doves and other accolades, I must admit there was a feeling of discontentment in my spirit. I kept remembering the early years of my career when I would sing a cappella—songs like "Peter, Don't Be Afraid," "Teach Me, Master, Teach Me," and "Satan,

We're Going to Tear Your Kingdom Down"—and I missed that old traditional gospel sound. And I believed that many of my older listeners did too. Without a doubt, it is those old traditional songs that seem to minister to your spirit and soul. Now with this new sound my record company had introduced me to in songs like "You Gotta Serve Somebody," "Glad You Came My Way," and "Sailin'," I felt I was only entertaining my audience. I was disturbed in my spirit. It caused me to reflect back to an incident that occurred while I was with Roadshow Records.

One day a lady called me long distance and said, "I am disappointed that you would record the songs on this *First Lady* album. This music is too worldly and will cause the people to pop their fingers to it."

She said, "As I began to play the album, I removed it from my record player and broke it!"

And then she said, "By the way, I know of a gospel announcer who did the same thing right over the air."

I thought for a moment and then said, "Well, if you can get past the music, just maybe you can hear the message." However, after I hung up the phone, I thought, Should she really have to do that—get past the music to hear the message?

Now here I was facing the same kind of dilemma, so I decided to do what I always did when there is turmoil in my mind and spirit. I went to talk to Mama. My mother was from the old school. She enjoyed traditional gospel music, the old hymns like "Amazing Grace" and "Precious Lord."

She was in the kitchen sitting at the table. And I mentioned that I was about to record another album. She said, "I will be so glad when you go back to singing like you used to sing, singing those old songs."

My reply was, "My company is trying to introduce me

to a broader audience in order to increase the distribution of my albums so that they will be sold not only in the mom-and-pop record shops, but also in Bible bookstores, Kmart stores, and other large music chains."

Mama said, "I don't care. I want my old Shirley back, the way she used to sing."

Her words stayed with me. "I want the old Shirley back. Sing the songs that bless the people."

Deep down I knew Mama was right. Whatever else happened, I had to sing the songs that I felt would bless the people. That is not to say that the songs I had been singing were bad songs. They weren't. The lyrics were strong gospel lyrics. But the style was new and, in many ways, was just not characteristic of me. And my listeners just were not ready for the new-sounding Shirley. I promised Mama that I would in fact go back to the old Shirley.

After that talk with my mother, I went ahead and recorded my next album, *Celebration,* in the summer of 1985. It included more songs that Mama didn't particularly like and that I felt uncomfortable with, but because we had already planned this album, I felt compelled to do it.

That fall, while I was out of town in concert, my mother suffered a mild stroke. I had not called home all that day because we were en route from Dothan, Alabama, to Mobile.

Late that evening I felt a compulsion to call home to speak with my husband. When he answered the phone, he said, "Shirley, where in the world have you all been? Why haven't you called? Mama suffered a mild stroke today, and she's in Duke Medical Center."

I immediately called my sister Anne, who was there with me, to the phone. My legs became so weak that while she was talking to my husband, a member of my group, Bernard Sterling, had to help me sit down.

After we hung up the phone, Anne and I simultaneously said, "We're going home."

I don't remember what time it was, but I do know that we had to ride all night long from Dotham, Alabama, to Atlanta, Georgia, to catch a 6:00 flight the following morning.

When we got off the plane, the two of us went straight to the hospital to our mother's bedside.

I walked in the room and over to her bed. I said, "Mama, do you know who I am?"

And she said, "You know I know who you are. You're Shirley."

As I stood there, all I could hear was the vow I had made to her: "I'm going back to the old Shirley." I knew that I would have to confront Word Records, but right then it just didn't matter at all. I was going back to doing what I did best: singing traditional gospel, maybe with a somewhat contemporary flavor.

And that's what I did. A few weeks later, I met with the top executives at Word to discuss my future with them. I knew I was at a crossroads, and that the outcome of that day would determine my direction for years to come, possibly for life.

By that time, Word had assigned me to their black gospel label, Rejoice, and they wanted to find a way to translate my popularity into more record sales. They asked me, "Shirley, what do you think you need? What will it take to break out into a broader market?"

As you would imagine, I had a ready answer for them, the answer from Mama. I said, "I need to get back to my roots. Let me record live with a choir, let me minister, let me be me."

"Is that really what you want to do?" they asked.

"Yes," I said, with eagerness in my voice. "Let me record a live album where I can respond to the crowd's reaction and be spontaneous."

I could tell they were thinking hard.

"Look," I said, "I know this will take some courage from both of us. But we have tried presenting Shirley Caesar in a contemporary style. We have used the studio musicians, even the professional background singers. We have dotted every *i* and crossed every *t*. But true gospel isn't done that way. I have got to be free to improvise, to be creative. That is what I do best. Anything that moves me away from that hurts me more than it helps."

Well, that talk convinced them. We went to work and made it happen. Working with Bubba Smith, my coproducer, we recorded *Live in Chicago*. I don't know when I have worked so hard but had so much fun. I told Bubba, "I want the Thompson Community Singers to back me on this project."

But not everything went well as we tried to make that album. For some reason, we had a lot of trouble getting the right songs for the project. It just seemed we couldn't get everything in place. Before we knew it, the deadline had come and several of the songs still weren't completed. In fact, on the very day of the live recording session, at least two of the ten songs were still in the writing stage.

Not knowing what else to do, I asked Darius Brooks, a writer for the Thompson Community Singers, if we could go somewhere to continue working on the songs. And he suggested his father's church.

As my musical director, Michael Mathis, Darius, and I were practicing, a young man, Reverend Donald Alfred, walked in off the street. I thought he was part of the choir. After a few minutes, he came up to me and told me he had a song for me.

I was skeptical because people try that all the time. But then I remembered a little girl trying something similar with Albertina Walker and the Caravans at a concert in North Carolina back in 1958. So I reviewed the song. Would you believe it, that song was exactly what I believed we needed. It was titled "Things Are Going to Get Better Some Day."

I was overjoyed.

But we still weren't finished. We needed one more song. We searched and searched and worked and worked, but nothing seemed to fit. Finally, tired and frustrated, we gave up, packed our equipment, and headed for the door.

Just as we were leaving, Michael turned, walked back to the organ, and sat down. I turned to see what he was doing.

He stared back at me and said, "Shirley, I believe the Lord is giving you a song to add to the story 'Hold My Mule.'" I just stood there for a second, trying to listen, trying to hear what the Lord was saying.

Michael played a chord on the organ. I said, "Give me an E-flat."

Out of nowhere I started singing. "I feel like praising, praising Him, praise Him in the morning, praise Him all day long, I feel like praising, praising Him." The words just began to flow out of me. Just like that the Lord had given us what we needed. By the time we finished singing, the song became "Hold My Mule." We recorded it that same night. I was a little uncertain about it, so I put it last on the repertoire of songs I would sing.

Given all that last-minute preparation, you can understand why I felt nervous that night. As we stood backstage at Christ's Tabernacle Church in Chicago, I stood in expectation of how the Lord would move that night. I felt good because I knew I was doing the right thing. I was fulfilling

Mama's last wish for me, and I was returning to my true gospel roots.

To say the least, the night and the album proved to be a tremendous success. "His Blood" became the most powerful song of the night, and the album soared almost immediately.

Live in Chicago dominated *Billboard*'s gospel chart for almost all of 1989, staying number one on their charts for fifty weeks. It sold an average of twenty-five thousand copies a week during that time and became Word's best-selling true gospel album. In addition, it won my fifth and sixth Dove Awards, one in the Traditional Black Gospel Album category and a single from it, "Hold My Mule," for Best Traditional Black Gospel Recorded Song. "Hold My Mule" also crossed over into the country music charts just as "No Charge" had done in earlier years. Though it didn't win a Grammy, it did propel me once again to the top of the industry. More than that, it took me back to my traditional style. Thank you, Word, for allowing my mother's dreams to become a reality.

One difficult thing about an album as successful as *Live in Chicago* is that it is very hard to top it. As that year ended and I met with my producers, they didn't quite know what to do for an encore. But the Lord took care of that. I knew exactly what he wanted me to do, and that was an album in memory of my mother.

The first couple of years after her demise, I found it very difficult to sing songs about mothers, and I certainly couldn't sing about mine. Even when we began planning my next live album, I still couldn't. But one day not too long after that, I sat down in my studio at home with Anne, Michael, Bernard, and the other Caesar Singers. Inadvertently, we started talking about Mama. Everyone told favorite stories about her— the way she fed us, the way she hugged us, the way she disciplined us, the way she prayed. For a long time that day and into the night, we sat and remembered the good things, the happy times.

I said to Anne, "Since we remember Mama in such a special way, why don't we write a song and entitle it 'I Remember Mama.'"

Well, that thought continuously stayed on my mind. I started playing around with the idea, and out of it emerged the song. That single cut became an instant hit, as did the entire album, which was also titled *I Remember Mama*. O'Landa Draper and the Associates of Memphis, Tennessee, backed us on the project. It was dedicated to Mama's memory. I believe she would have been pleased.

To complement that release, I did something new and innovative. I recorded a concept video based on the title cut of the album. This was during the time when the whole concept of religious videos was in the beginning stages. We filmed it at the Simmons Street house where I grew up. Many family members—brothers and sisters, nieces and nephews— came together to participate in it. My oldest sister, Lucille Caesar Spencer, who looked exactly like my mother, portrayed Mama. If you've seen Lucille in that video, you've seen my mama. Little did we know that this film, which was intended as a tribute to my mother, would also become a legacy to Lucille, for she died shortly thereafter.

We shot the video the day after Christmas. The weather was overcast and bitterly cold. I was so cold that I put on a big sweater under the suit I was wearing. Everybody bundled up. We would shoot a scene and then run into the house to warm up. If you look closely on the video you can see vapors coming out of our mouths as we sang. The concept of the video was to depict the day I received Christ into my life in the backyard of that same house as we were playing church. It was intended as a promotional item for the album, but because of its popularity and impact, Word Records decided to market it as a stand-alone feature. It sold so well that it became a certified gold video.

During the eighties, returning to my traditional gospel roots and reshaping my music career occupied a large segment of my time, but I was also extremely busy completing my formal education, building my ministry, and beginning to serve as copastor, and later pastor, of a local church.

After I married Bishop Williams, I became more and more involved with him in his ministry both in the national and local church body. This proved to be invaluable to my ministry, for I wanted to prepare myself for the pastorate. I knew the Lord was calling me into that field of ministry, and I knew the best method of preparation was to be my husband's copastor.

As if that wasn't enough, and in addition to everything else, in 1987 I decided to run for the City Council of Durham.

I know that's a bit unusual for a minister. When I started talking about it, a number of people tried to discourage me. "You won't have time," some of them said. "Politicians are crooked," a few of them suggested. "It'll hurt your career," offered one or two. Many of the church people said, "Politics and religion don't mix."

But I didn't listen. Not only was Jesus the greatest politician in the world because he dealt directly with people and with their problems, but Joseph became the prime minister of Egypt. If God could use a Joseph in the political arena, why not a Christian servant? I believe that the political system needs born-again believers in office and serving in the highest positions in the land.

I'd been thinking about running for office for years. I wanted to do my part for the city where I grew up. It had always meant so much to me, and I wanted to give back to my community. I thank the Lord for people like Lavonia Allison and Willie Lovett who encouraged me.

I believed I knew what the people needed as well as what they wanted. I knew how to get out, roll up my sleeves, and go to work to make my town one of equal opportunity for everyone.

I started my campaign, running for one of three at-large positions on the city council. As many of you know, when I do something I try to do it with all my heart. I do it to win. I don't want to fail. Consequently, I worked hard in the campaign.

Having taken some marketing courses while completing my undergraduate studies at Shaw University, I knew a little about advertising strategy. We devised a campaign to make sure the people knew that Shirley Caesar sincerely cared about the welfare of others.

We printed thousands of flyers to distribute door-to-door. And we printed hundreds of placards. My friends, campaign workers, and Boy Scout Troop #55 distributed the flyers and posted the placards everywhere—on trees, on telephone poles, in windows.

The flyers listed my platform (which was also on the back of the campaign card pictured in the photo section). I believed that:

- No Durham citizen needed to be unemployed.
- No Durham citizen needed to be without proper care and protection.
- No Durham citizen needed to be without public transportation.
- Durham's downtown did not need to die while Raleigh and RTP (Research Triangle Park) were infused with economic life.

- Durham's neighborhoods needed to be preserved. And Durham's environment needed protection.

Artis Plummer Signs, a local business enterprise, built us a huge wooden pyramid sign to hook onto a flatbed trailer. Each side of the sign read: VOTE FOR SHIRLEY CAESAR.

One evening we went to a campaign rally at Saint Mark AME Church. At the end of the rally, Carolyn Sanders, my campaign manager, Melvinia Parker, and another friend left the parking lot to drive back to my house.

As they proceeded down Fayetteville Street, the sign started to come apart, board by board. My prayer partner and sister in the Lord, Melvinia, got out of the car and onto the flatbed truck, between the pyramid signs, trying to hold them together.

Carolyn was driving very slow, about five to ten miles an hour, and Melvinia was constantly hollering, "Slow down. Slow down. It's falling apart."

They were hilarious to watch. Watching them was better than watching a parade. People were doubled over in laughter as they passed, but they got the message to vote for Shirley Caesar.

The next day we took the sign back to Art Plummer and had him tighten it on the truck.

Not everything that happened during the campaign was quite that funny. One morning, Bishop Williams and I went out to put up some campaign signs in neighborhood yards and on street corners. As we were working, we looked back and saw a young man coming along behind us pulling up our signs.

As you can imagine, we were disturbed by his actions. My husband decided to find out why the man was doing this. We pulled up beside him on the road. Bishop Williams asked, "What are you doing taking down those signs?"

The man said, "Someone told me to do it."

Bishop asked him, "Who?"

But he wouldn't say. Just that someone paid him to do it. We told him to leave the signs alone. He did, at least as long as we were there.

We had a few other negatives also to arise during the campaign. *The Phil Donahue Show* had scheduled me to appear some months prior to my deciding to run for a public office. Days before my scheduled appearance his staff called and said they needed to postpone. They explained that if they allowed me to appear, they would have to afford the same opportunity to my opponents.

Given that kind of situation, we worked extra hard to win. We purchased newspaper ads, put up billboards, did all the things a candidate running for office is expected to do, and then some.

A number of groups endorsed me—the Durham Committee on the Affairs of Black People, the People's Alliance, and the Durham Voters Alliance. I owe a word of thanks to those groups.

Finally election night came. The culmination of all our hard work was soon to be realized. All of my family and friends gathered at my mother's house to watch the election. We watched part of the returns on television, but as the precincts began closing we gathered at the election board office for the final results. As the numbers were tallied in my favor, I kept hugging my friends, clapping my hands, and jumping up and down. When all of the precinct results were in, I couldn't believe it. I had won! I couldn't believe we had accomplished what the vote was indicating. I had won an election in a southern city by 68 percent of the vote. In fact, African Americans filled all three at-large seats on the council. The other two winners were Peggy Watson-Borden and

Johnny "Red" Williams. But the most phenomenal accomplishment of the election was that eight out of thirteen city council members elected that year were African Americans, the first time in Durham's history. That fact demonstrated just how far the South had come and just how far the Lord had brought me.

My immediate goals as an elected official were to fulfill my campaign promises: to provide affordable housing for the elderly, to decrease unemployment, and to promote the return of business to the downtown area. I also wanted to recruit more business and industry to our city. As I told a reporter from the *The Herald-Sun*, "There are only so many jobs in Durham. We have to get more jobs to come to us."

When you really think about it, it is still ministry to serve in politics, because I'm helping to make my city a better place. I believe Jesus wants me to do that. My ministry is what inspired me to run for office. I felt I had been dealing with a lot of problems on the surface for years, but by stepping into the fray, by going behind the scenes, by sitting at the table where decisions that affected lives are made, I believed I could make a difference.

Everyone asked me where I would find the time to serve on the council. The council met twice a month, and I had to find time to study the issues and attend functions. It wasn't easy. I had to forfeit several engagements to make the meetings.

Once, I attended a meeting on crutches. That morning I had been in Boston attending the funeral of Michael Mathis's father. At the funeral, I had fallen down a flight of steps, from the top all the way to the bottom. It's a wonder I didn't break my neck. As I lay there, I couldn't even feel my ankle. I tried to stand up but couldn't.

A man I didn't even know picked me up. I was taken to

the emergency room where my ankle was x-rayed. It wasn't broken, but it wasn't far from it. The doctor wrapped it up, put me on crutches, and sent me home.

That night in Durham, my ankle aching badly, I thought about staying home from the council meeting, but I couldn't do it. The people had elected me to represent them, so I hobbled into the council meeting.

For four years I poured myself into that job, just as I've poured myself into every other job I've ever tried to do. Every day that I served on city council, I learned something new. I didn't care how anyone else on the council voted. I voted my convictions. Other council members said later that I brought sensitivity to the council that hadn't been there before. I appreciated their saying that.

More than anything, I wanted people to know I was more than a gospel singer, more than a preacher. I not only care about what happens inside the church; I'm equally concerned about what happens in society at large. In my opinion, if the church doesn't influence society, it has failed to live out God's commission.

At the end of one term, four years, I felt led to relinquish my seat on the council, because at that point my ministry had surpassed singing and evangelizing and I was fulfilling my commission to pastor.

I'm so committed to whatever I do that I don't like to feel something is suffering because I am too stressed out. I could probably have remained, but something would have suffered—my church or my council seat or my singing or my husband. And I couldn't let that happen.

CHAPTER ELEVEN

Ministry to the World

THE MELODY

I've got a message God gave me for the nation
This is a message to warn men of their sins
He told me to tell you that Jesus is coming
He's coming back with a reward in His hand
He's coming like a thief and a robber in the night
If I were you, my brother, I would get my business right
When Jesus comes, my friend, you won't have no place to run
The reason you won't serve Him, you're too busy having fun
I've got a message I've got to give to the nation
—"Message to the Nation"

AND THE WORD

For the Lord Himself will descend from heaven with a shout,
with the voice of an archangel, and with the trumpet of God.
And the dead in Christ will rise first.
Then we who are alive and remain shall be caught up
together with them in the clouds to meet the Lord in the air.
And thus we shall always be with the Lord.
—1 Thessalonians 4:16–17

—— THE Lord has opened a countless number of wonderful doors through which I have entered to speak a word of faith to thousands. Many of the people to whom I am privileged to minister in word and song are generally the ordinary people who keep the world running—blue-collar workers, hairdressers, carpenters, schoolteachers, grocery store clerks, nurses, housewives, and children. They attend my revivals and concerts and acquire my recordings to hear some words of encouragement that will keep them persevering, believing, and hoping the Lord will impart to them the strength and stamina needed to make it through another day.

There is also another group of people who listen to my music, and I'm very grateful that they do. They are individuals who occupy special positions accompanied by special burdens. They find themselves in unique places—influential places from which they can shape opinions and effect change. Some are politicians, others are entertainers, and still others are activists and advocates. They are subjected to intense scrutiny, and they often lead lonely lives full of responsibility. And they need encouragement like everyone else.

Whenever the Lord has opened the door for me to witness and encourage many of the world's leading citizens, I have always tried to be spontaneous and spiritually ready to minister.

Part of our charge and divine commission as Christians is to "go into the highways and byways and compel men and women to come to Jesus." Consequently I've always been one to witness on a daily basis to anyone and everyone. I realized the urgency of doing this as far back as 1963, when I had the opportunity of witnessing about Jesus to Sam Cooke, a former lead singer of the Soul Stirrers, of Chicago, Illinois.

As a young teenager I loved and admired the Soul Stirrers; they had such a unique style of singing. I was particularly fascinated by the voice quality of one of their lead singers, a young man named Sam Cooke. Sam had such magnificent voice control, smooth and melodious. His yodels and runs were like none you ever heard. Unlike the yodels you hear in country western music, Sam's were refined, unruffled, and polished. He was simply awesome! No one could sing like Sam Cooke, but I tried to emulate him. Every musical run he made, I felt I could make it. I even thought I could yodel like him. I remember Cassietta George telling me that Sam had taught her how to yodel, and she could really sing. I tried to sing his songs just as he would sing them, particularly "Nearer My God to Thee" and "Touch the Hem of His Garment." However, everybody knows that there was only one Sam Cooke.

After I joined the Caravans, there were many times when we appeared on the same concert with the Soul Stirrers, and we all became friends. Sam was a wonderful person and was a lot of fun to be around, very playful. He eventually left the Soul Stirrers and began a career in R & B. In the secular world he was noted for such songs as "Darling, You Send Me" and "I Love You for Sentimental Reasons."

One day while the Caravans were singing in Los Angeles, I ran into Sam. We had lost contact after he left the Soul Stirrers, and I hadn't seen him in years. I didn't know about his walk with the Lord, but I felt a strong compulsion to talk to him about Jesus. He listened to me as I told him about Jesus, seeming to pay attention to what I had to say. When I finished he asked, "Shirley, can't you talk about anything except Jesus and God?"

"Sure, but what's more important to talk about?"

"I don't know, but that's all you do, talk about Jesus."

"Jesus is the most important thing to me, and He should be to you also."

Sam was a real comedian; he loved to play all of the time. And of course he laughed his way right out of our conversation.

I don't know if Sam took what I said to heart. I'm not even sure if what I said did any good, but tragically, less than two weeks later, Sam Cooke was dead, shot and killed. When that happened, it reminded me again that regardless of how famous, rich, or powerful one may be, our days are numbered and it is imperative that we all are in right standing with the Lord.

From whatever platform the Lord makes available, and from whatever door He opens, I always take the opportunity to present Jesus.

In 1979 I received an invitation from President Jimmy Carter to sing at the White House along with the Richard Smallwood Singers and the Mighty Clouds of Joy. While sitting on the White House lawn, President and Mrs. Carter told me they enjoyed gospel music and that they, in fact, owned some of my albums. I knew they both were raised in an evangelical church.

When it was my turn to sing, I turned and asked, "Mr. President, do you know what this country needs?"

He said, "I have my own ideas, but you tell me what you think the country needs."

I said, "This country needs a miracle." And then I sang "Miracle Worker." I'll never forget that wonderful evening of sharing gospel music right there on the White House lawn.

I've since had other opportunities to sing at the White House. Each time I've been invited, I've made every effort to go. It doesn't matter whether a person is a Republican or a Democrat; I deem it an honor to carry a testimony of the

Lord to those in power and leadership. I constantly pray for the leaders of our country; no one can imagine the stress and pressure they endure.

In February of 1992 I returned to the White House to sing for President George Bush. In celebration of Black History Month he had invited Maya Angelou, Colin Powell, Clarence Thomas, Benjamin Hooks, and myself along with two hundred other guests to join him and Mrs. Bush in the East Room of the White House. Following Maya Angelou's recital of poetry commemorating Black History, I sang "Steal Away to Jesus," an old Negro spiritual, and President Bush delivered a very inspirational speech that transcended political affiliation. In listening to him it was immaterial that I was Democratic and he Republican.

I kept a copy of President Bush's speech because it challenged all of us to move beyond our racial prejudices.

He said,

> There is not, and there never will be, a place in America for hatred, for prejudice, for intolerance. Let's push back the small crowds who preach hatred. Let's create room for the American Dream—and for a land where all God's children sing in the joyous songs of freedom. And so that's our challenge. And I hope it will form the next chapter of our national history.

In speaking of black leaders like labor leader A. Philip Randolph and civil rights leader Rosa Parks, the president said, "These pioneers, and many like them, peered over the rim of the possible and dared to walk where others had only dreamed."

In his words, America stood on "the edge of a frontier—the frontier of brotherhood and a better tomorrow. It's up to us to see beyond old divides and set our sights on new common ground. As we continue our efforts to create prosperity for all, we must also create a new trust, a new tolerance, and a new opportunity. And we will."

Those words say what we all need to hear. America, and the world for that matter, needs to get past the old stereotypes that keep us apart and move on to the love of the Lord that will bring us together.

We certainly have enough to tear us apart. In every area of life we see troubles and problems, divisions and accusations. We live in a time when everyone wants to tear everyone else down. I see my ministry as that of trying to build other people up and to be a repairer of the breach.

I feel honored that many people from all walks of life have been blessed by my music and my ministry and have asked me to pray for them. I've had the privilege of sharing prayers and words of testimony with both Clarence Thomas and Michael Jackson. (And I love them both.)

The hearings to determine whether or not Clarence Thomas would become a member of the U.S. Supreme Court were not only a dark and trying time for him and his family, but they were also a dreadful time for our country and the black community. I didn't know it then, but later I received a handwritten note from Supreme Court Justice Clarence Thomas telling me how my music had ministered to him during that grim period in his life. In that note, he told me,

> As I sit here listening to your inspirational music, I'm so grateful for your work. You have had a great impact on me as I have tried to do God's will. For all you have done and all the help and guidance you have given me on my walk, I thank you.

Later I visited with him in his office, along with my friend Armstrong Williams. We talked for several minutes, then shared a time of prayer together. I asked the Lord to give him guidance to make wise decisions, to give him strength to endure hard days, to help him remember his faith.

When Michael Jackson asked me to sing with him on an album, a door was again opened for me to share my testimony of the Lord.

The Caesar Singers were invited to sing on the *Sunday Night Live* television program, along with Take 6 and the Dixie Hummingbirds. That night I remember singing the song "Lord, Let Your Spirit Fall on Me." The following week a representative from Michael Jackson's office called my office. She said that Mr. Jackson wanted to meet with me about recording a song with him on an upcoming project.

My manager, Carolyn Sanders, said, "Is this a joke?"

"No. This is very, very real. Mr. Jackson would like to meet with Miss Caesar."

I was scheduled to go to Los Angeles anyway for the Stellar Awards, so I decided to meet with Michael during that time. The meeting was scheduled for 2:30 in the afternoon. I was so excited about meeting Michael Jackson that I left my hotel early and went across the street to the Broadway Mall to kill some time. While browsing there, and carefully monitoring my watch, I suddenly felt a rumbling under my feet. Since I was on the seventh floor of the mall I thought perhaps it was the vibration of the huge trucks passing by. Still very nervous about meeting Michael, I went back to my hotel room and turned on the television. Every channel I tuned in was broadcasting the news of the terrible earthquake of 1989, which had just hit the Oakland-San Francisco Bay area. Immediately I knew that the rumbling I felt under my feet was the aftershock of the earthquake taking place in Northern California over three hundred and fifty miles away.

I became so engrossed in the newscast that my meeting with Michael Jackson became secondary. I looked at my watch. It was nearing 1:45, so I went downstairs, caught a taxi, and went to the studio address his representative had given me.

Arriving thirty minutes early, I went across the street to a doughnut shop and bought two jelly doughnuts and a container of orange juice. I walked back to the studio and was sitting there eating my snack when I noticed on the overhead monitor a long limousine pull up in the back driveway. Approximately ten minutes later, a man came in and told me Mr. Jackson had arrived.

I followed the gentleman into a room off from the studio. As we entered he asked, "Have you thought about how much you want to charge?"

I paused for a second. I hadn't even thought about money. I told him, "No, I haven't, I really just want to meet Michael Jackson."

I wanted to meet him because I admired his talent and versatility. He never sings a song the same way. I was thrilled that such a multitalented megastar would even consider asking me to share a song with him. There were just so many positive things about Michael Jackson that I admired, and I wanted to meet him.

A few minutes later Michael Jackson appeared, a long black cane in his hand, a hat on his head, and dark glasses over his eyes. He walked over to me to shake my hand. I smiled at him and shook my head. "Oh, no," I said. "You've got to hug me!"

He laughed and opened his arms, and we embraced. I said to him, "You're going to think this sounds crazy, but I've always called you my son."

He smiled and said, "I love you, and I love your work."

Of course I appreciated his comments. As we sat down together, his sound engineer began to set up the song that Michael wanted me to consider. I asked Michael how he had heard of me and why he wanted me of all people to sing with him.

"I saw you on *Sunday Night Live*," he said, "so I had one of my staff members call you."

He turned to his soundman. "Man, she's bad," he said, "I wouldn't want to follow her on stage."

I laughed with him. "No, you're the bad one," I said. "You're just extraordinary."

We talked about various topics, but of course music and singing were at the top of the list. Before either of us realized it, our conversation changed and we began talking about the Lord. I certainly didn't try to influence the conversation in that direction, but I didn't hesitate to say something for the Lord while I had the opportunity. Not wanting to sound as though I was preaching to him, I was very subtle in reminding him of how much the Lord loved him, how the Lord had blessed him, and how he had given him great talents. Michael later told me he appreciated the conversation.

A major manufacturing company (I think it was L.A. Gear) called the studio during the time of our meeting. Apparently they wanted to continue their discussion of the possibility of Michael endorsing their athletic shoes. The gentleman who greeted me when I arrived walked over to Michael and whispered in his ear that the company was on the telephone. Michael replied, "Take a number. We'll call them back."

"How do you handle all the demands on your life?" I asked. "It's hard for me, so I know it must be even harder for you. There are times when the demands are so overwhelming. How do you handle it?"

He thought for a second, then said, "You just say no."

I never forgot that.

Then he asked me, "What do you do for your hoarseness?"

I said, "The main thing is try to get some rest. But that's not always easy to do. What about you?"

He laughed. "I have a steam cup. I place my head over the cup and inhale the vapors. That sometimes seems to help."

The studio technicians played the tape of the song Michael wanted me to consider, but it didn't sound like something I'd sing. The name of it was "Earth," and it dealt with environmental issues. I guess I felt that way because he had only a rough taping of the song, but the finished product was awesome.

After listening to the song I said, "Am I to sing this along with you?"

He said yes. He wanted me to co-lead it with him.

A few minutes later, Andrae and Sandra Crouch came in and joined the meeting. They were also collaborating with Michael on the project. Andrae and Sandra and I are very good friends, and instantly he began playfully teasing me about my home state and city, saying that "she's from a little country town in North Carolina." But Michael rescued me from Andrae's teasing by saying exemplary things about North Carolina. The more Andrae teased me, the more Michael defended me. The moment Michael said "I remember traveling on the train through North Carolina when I was a little boy," a vague memory from years ago instantly came to mind. One Sunday morning a group of young male singers traveling through Durham, North Carolina, came to our church. A deacon in our church asked them, "What's the name of your group?"

The oldest one said, "You mean to tell me you don't know

who we are? We're the Jackson Five." So Michael Jackson had actually been to Durham, North Carolina, and worshiped in our church!

I didn't sing with Michael on that album. His production company was supposed to contact us again, but sadly enough, when the church world heard that I might sing with Michael Jackson, many became very critical and condemning. My office received an untold number of calls from people denouncing Michael Jackson and saying I shouldn't participate on any recording with him. A few people even started making jokes about it. My song "Hold My Mule" was very popular at the time, and people started saying, "Hold my mule while I sing with Michael Jackson."

When I heard those ugly and cruel remarks, I withdrew, deciding that even if Michael called again, I wouldn't be able to participate on the project.

I would have loved to work with Michael Jackson, because I saw in him a part of myself. As children neither of us had really been able to enjoy a normal childhood because we were always traveling and working, Michael even more so than myself. Consequently, I knew firsthand the loneliness and alienation he must have endured growing up. I would have really loved to be a friend to him, but he never called me back. Let the record show, however, that I love Michael Jackson, and I don't allow anyone to discuss him negatively in my presence.

Just as I have had the privilege of singing for President Carter and President Bush, I have also had the opportunity of singing for President Bill Clinton on two occasions. The first occasion was during the bicentennial celebration of the University of North Carolina where President Clinton was the keynote speaker, and I sang the national anthem. The second occasion was in 1996, at the Women's Leadership Forum in Washington, D.C. I'll never forget that occasion. Over three thousand women came together with Mrs. Clinton and Mrs. Gore to lend their support for the reelection of President Clinton and Vice President Al Gore. I was very pleased that the committee selected gospel as the music for the evening, and I was highly honored and humbled that they would invite me and the Caesar Singers to be the musical artists for the event. Even though the affair was held in the ballroom of the Hyatt Hotel, when we began to minister in song it felt as though we were in worship service at the Mount Calvary Holy Church where I pastor. Each time that I have sung for presidents, they have either asked me to pray for them or I have made it a point to tell them they are in my prayers.

I believe every citizen bears the responsibility of praying for our leaders in government. In fact, the Bible emphatically instructs us to do so. It is unfortunate that sometimes our attitude toward politics is so negative that we forget we can change this world through prayer. Yes, we have an inalienable right to protest the policies of politicians or political parties, but our method of protest should be prayer and the casting of our votes. Through prayer, great changes have been effected politically, socially, economically, and racially, not only in our nation but in other nations as well. If you really think about it, more change has been accomplished through prayer and supplication than by protest.

One of the greatest political transformations happened in the country of South Africa when the practice of apartheid was finally abolished after being imposed for decades. No longer were blacks and whites to be separated with the white minority ruling and the black majority in bondage. During those awful years of apartheid, Nelson Mandela dedicated his life to bringing an end to this practice. For twenty-seven years the South African government incarcerated him because of his stance against this oppressive system. But prison could not silence his voice, and people all over the world interceded in prayer continuously for him and the South African Nation.

Miraculously, conditions began to change. Some bloodshed occurred and many lives were lost. But it could have been far worse. Finally, in 1990, Mandela was freed and South Africans began the process of changing their country's political structure.

Shortly after his release, while touring the United States to raise funds for the African National Congress (ANC), Mandela traveled to Atlanta, Georgia, where a grand gala had been organized in his honor. June 27, 1990, stands out as a significant day for our nation and for me, for that was the day I had the pleasure of meeting Nelson Mandela and singing for him.

It had been hot all day—the temperature nearing ninety-five degrees. Thousands of people crowded the downtown area along Auburn Avenue, outside the famed Bethel Baptist Church and adjacent to the Martin Luther King Jr. Center for Social Change Memorial, and into Bobby Dodd Stadium, the home of the Georgia Tech football team. Thunderstorms rumbled through the sky for much of the afternoon. Mandela's appearance ran two hours behind schedule, but no one seemed to mind. People had waited twenty-seven years to see and to hear this man speak. Two more hours were seconds in comparison. Everyone had come to celebrate this historical moment. Not since Dr. Martin Luther King Jr. had one man inspired so many people.

Over fifty thousand people gathered in the stadium for a combination concert, inspirational rally, and freedom celebration. I was ecstatic to be a part of this celebration. A host of other musicians from every style—reggae, jazz, pop, soul, and gospel—were performing on the stage that day. Peabo

Bryson traveled all the way from Jamaica, and Hugh Masekela, a composer and trumpeter, had come from South Africa. Ten years old, Tiombe Lockhart left us in tears when she sang "To Dream the Impossible Dream."

As I began to sing, I stared out over the crowd. A sea of green and gold—the colors of the African National Congress, Mandela's political party—waved back at me in the summer air. I couldn't help but think of how God had answered the prayers of all those who had prayed for Nelson Mandela's release from prison and for the abolition of apartheid. I thought about what a privilege it is to live in America. It is not a perfect nation, but we are highly favored of the Lord. With those thoughts in mind, I sang three songs, "The Star Spangled Banner," "Precious Lord," and "Amazing Grace." Mandela had personally requested "Precious Lord."

Mandela's speech inspired and thrilled everyone. He said, "I'm here in Atlanta today because I support the struggle for freedom. So let freedom ring. Let freedom ring wherever the people's rights are trampled upon."

Thousands of heads nodded in agreement as he spoke. In America we have more freedom than any other country, but even here we haven't reached the Promised Land. Even here, we have a long way to go.

As the sun set that evening, I closed the ceremony with "Amazing Grace." I sang the song with a renewed knowledge of just how amazing God's grace really was. Here before us had stood a man who had spent the last twenty-seven years of his life in prison, and if left up to man he would have spent the remainder of his life there. But God had provided for his freedom, and Mandela would become the president of the very country that had imprisoned him. If that isn't amazing grace, then what is? When the program closed and the people had begun to stream out of the stadium, Mandela gave me one of the greatest compliments I've ever received. He took my hand and said, "During my time in prison, tapes of the sermons of Martin Luther King Jr. and tapes of the songs of Shirley Caesar kept me going. When I got really discouraged, I listened to your music. It helped me remember that God loved me and would see me through."

My philosophy in life has always been, "Christ first, others second, myself last." Thus, if I can help somebody as I travel along—Nelson Mandela and any other person—I've fulfilled God's purpose for my life.

CHAPTER TWELVE

Ministry as a Pastor

THE MELODY

*Though the pressures of life seem to weigh you down
and you don't know which way to turn
God is concerned, and He's working it out for you.
The child that's on cocaine
through prayer he can change
that marriage that's on the verge of breaking up
Although sometimes we have to walk all alone
You ask yourself is there a word from the Lord
You need a blessing and you need it right away
God is concerned, and He is working it out for you.
No peace in the home
There's no peace on the job
the bills are due and your health is failing too.
God is concerned, and He's working it out for you.*
—"He's Working It Out for You"

AND THE WORD

*And I, brethren, when I came to you,
did not come with excellence of speech or of wisdom*

declaring to you the testimony of God.
For I determined not to know anything among you
except Jesus Christ and Him crucified.
I was with you in weakness, in fear, and in much trembling.
And my speech and my preaching were not
with persuasive words of human wisdom,
but in demonstration of the Spirit and of power.
—1 Corinthians 2:1–4

———— FROM the day I married, I began to minister alongside my husband, who, in addition to being the pastor of the local Mount Calvary Holy Church in Winston-Salem, North Carolina, is also the senior bishop of the Mount Calvary Holy Churches of America. For seven years I served in the capacity of copastor, performing all the duties of a pastor, including visiting the sick, teaching Bible study, preaching sermons, administering the Lord's Supper, performing weddings, and counseling married couples, young women, and even young men who had drifted into drugs. Little did I know then that the Lord was preparing me for the pastorate that he would later assign me to in Raleigh, North Carolina.

I knew before I accepted the Lord in my life at age twelve that my destiny was to be a minister of the gospel of Jesus Christ. Therefore, at age seventeen, when I heard the voice of the Lord calling me into ministry, I readily said yes! Yet, never in my wildest dreams did I think I would ever pastor my own church.

People often tell me that I have the heart of a pastor. Presumably, their perception derives from the fact that I genuinely love God's people. If it were in my power, there wouldn't be any sick, hurting, hungry, or homeless people. Although

I realize it is impossible for me to eradicate these conditions completely, I try with everything that is within me to alleviate them to some degree. Whenever and wherever I can demonstrate concern, offer prayer, and provide food, clothing, and shelter to those in need, I don't hesitate to do so. People who find it hard to believe that a person can be earnestly concerned about the welfare of others often question my actions. Thinking I have an ulterior motive, they ask, "What do you have up your sleeve?" I tell them, "My arm!" I just know that helping others is a viable component of being a minister of Jesus Christ.

In concerts I'm introduced as "Evangelist Shirley Caesar," because whether in church services or concert performances, I'm on a mission to "reach the lost at any cost." Given this perspective of ministry, I guess I should have perceived inevitably that the Lord would, in His timing, elevate me to the pastorate.

It's very difficult for women to be received as preachers, but acceptance is even more difficult for women who pastor. The opposition coming from those who believe women should neither preach nor pastor is unbelievable. You find resistance in both black and white churches. In times past it was even worse. The consensus was that as long as women in the ministry referred to themselves as *evangelists, missionaries,* or *teachers,* they were, for the most part, received in the churches, but if they ventured to call themselves *preachers* or *pastors,* they were very often prohibited from ministering in many churches. And if permitted to minister, they could not preach from the pulpit as male preachers were allowed to do. They had to deliver their sermons from behind a table on the floor. The belief seemed to have been that the gospel was not the gospel unless a man was delivering it. Sadly enough, much of this same school of thought persists today. But my response to such thinking is, "If God can trust a woman to carry His living Word, as Mary carried the baby Jesus in her womb, certainly God can also trust a woman to carry His written Word in her life as a preacher and pastor."

On more than one occasion, I've encountered situations where I've been discriminated against as a female minister. Once I was invited to speak at a large church in Newark, New Jersey. I was unaware of this church's stance against women preachers, therefore when I was escorted to a seat among the general assembly I simply thought this was a temporary position and they would later invite me to the pulpit. Of course, that never occurred. Upon my introduction, the ushers placed a table on the floor in front of the pulpit and motioned for me to come. I realized then that I was kindly being told that I was not welcome in their pulpit. My first inclination was to retaliate, but then I decided not to say anything. Instead, I thanked them for their kind introduction, pulled the table back into the corner, and proceeded to deliver my sermon. This wasn't the first time I'd been confronted with situations of this sort, and it wouldn't be the last. After all, it really didn't matter from where I spoke as long as the message was heard.

In 1996 on another occasion, I accompanied my musician, Michael Mathis, to the home-going celebration of his former pastor, Elder E. I. Osborne, in Boston, Massachusetts. The family had requested that I sing and have words of expression at the funeral, which was being held at a larger church to accommodate those in attendance. As it would happen, that church also didn't recognize women preachers or pastors. Although the family had specifically requested that I speak to the congregation, I was again denied the privilege of sitting in the pulpit along with the male preachers. Once again I sang and spoke from the floor.

When these kinds of incidents occur, I refuse to get upset.

After all, I want to epitomize what I preach. If I preach forgiveness, I must practice forgiving. My response for such situations is, "The same Jesus who speaks from behind the pulpit also speaks from behind the table on the floor." The truth of the matter is that Jesus spoke from everywhere except from behind a pulpit desk. He used an old ship, a mountaintop, and even a desert for a pulpit. He certainly didn't need the confines of a church to make His point, and neither do I. It doesn't matter if I'm ministering in a tent, an outdoor stadium, or a cathedral, for God uses whomever he chooses, regardless of gender or race.

It's unfortunate that people get caught up in tradition and rituals and forget what God's Word says. I know there are some who make their case against women preachers from the biblical passage about women keeping silent in the church, but that is grossly taken out of context. In Scripture after Scripture we find women leading the people of God. If you want to be technical about it, women became the first preachers after the resurrection when Jesus told them specifically to "go and tell" others what they had seen and heard. The truth of the matter is that women were last at the cross and first at the tomb.

When I hear someone say they don't believe in women preachers, I tell them, "I don't believe in *women* preachers either, and neither do I believe in *men* preachers. I believe in Spirit-filled preachers." In essence, it's not the man or the woman, but the Holy Spirit who ultimately does the preaching. If the Holy Spirit isn't at work, it doesn't matter what gender stands behind the sacred pulpit. Accordingly, if the Holy Ghost is at work, the same is true, man or woman, the message will be received.

It has been said that I'm one of the pioneers of women in the ministry, and I think that is exciting. I believe this view of me arises from the fact that I was the first woman evangelist to record a sermon, "Go Take a Bath," with a major record label and also from the fact that at the time God called me into ministry there were very few women preachers evangelizing our nation, especially among African Americans. Aside from such gospel greats as Emily Braham, Ardell Tucker, Rosie Wallace, Lettie Cohen, Annie Pearl Hairston, Ethel Williams, and Ernestine Reems, there were few others. And I feel quite privileged to be named among them.

I've often heard ministers say that when God called them to ministry they fought against it, but I never ran from my calling. I always wanted to sing and preach and pray for the sick. In my early teens I wanted to be used of God so badly that I would lie in bed and visualize myself praying for masses of people who were sick, and my mother was always first in the prayer line. I guess I wanted her to be healed so badly, I would actually dream of her running and leaping, completely healed. That dream never came true, at least not in this life, but my singing and preaching the gospel certainly did.

I am a minister by divine calling and a pastor by divine appointment, and my determination is to fulfill this charge God has placed upon my life. I am not one to give up easily. Even as a child I had a stubborn streak in me. Time after time, I insisted on having the last word. My mother would tell me to stop talking, and I would mumble, "But I wasn't talking." When she rightfully accused me of doing something, I would still whisper, "But I didn't do it." The stubbornness that came out as a child's rebellion is now an adult's determination.

I believe "*determination* is the strongest nation in the world." When I am told that I can't, it is then that I determine I can and I will! Discouragement is a spirit; you can't see it, but you can see the effects of it. If you allow it to take you over, it will overtake you. If I had listened to the negative things said about me and to me and against me, I would have given up long ago. But I am not a quitter. I believe I can stand any test, for "If God is for us, who can be against us?" I refuse to be discouraged. I will not falter under the pressure of the enemy, because giving up is, in essence, denying my call to the ministry, and I know emphatically that I am chosen of God to minister in this twentieth and twenty-first century.

The enemy has tried time and time again to destroy my ministry, knowing that if I retreat he could circumvent the ministry of thousands of other young men and women who feel the call of God on their lives. Thus, I must press forward. I know that if I can make the road they must travel a little easier and open doors that would otherwise be shut, then I've accomplished part of what the Lord has commissioned me to do.

Although the resistance against women preachers and pastors is still prevalent among some denominations, the situation is improving every day. Today, because of the pioneers who blazed trails along the way, there are now a number of women evangelists who are sweeping the country with the gospel of Jesus Christ, evangelists such as Iona Locke, Jackie McCullough, Maria Gardner, Juanita Bynum, Arlene Churn, Debra Lockett Graham, Claudette Copeland, Barbara Amos, Juanita Sapp, and the list goes on and on. The church is blessed in that we've progressed beyond tradition and have focused on the real issue, winning souls for the kingdom.

My ministry takes precedence in my life, and that involves total commitment to my church. I endeavor to serve my congregation with all diligence and to avail myself to address their spiritual and natural needs. Although weekends are prime days for gospel concerts, I make every concentrated effort to be in our pulpit each Sunday morning. There have been times when I have been in concert as far away as California and have caught a red-eye special to fly all night to get back to Raleigh, North Carolina, in time for our morning worship service. More times than I can remember I've arrived at the airport as late as 10:00 A.M., rushed home to shower and dress, and have driven to church, arriving just in time for the 11:00 A.M. service. There have even been times when I've had to fly out again, after morning service, to get to a Sunday night concert.

There are instances, however, when it is virtually impossible for me to get a flight home in time for worship service. When that occurs, and I am thankful that it isn't often, I don't despair even though I long to be there. God has placed in Mount Calvary some wonderful preachers—Evangelist Carolyn Sanders, Bishop Ocie Gorham, Evangelist Wynita Taylor, Elder Tommy Mays, and many others—to minister in my absence. From time to time my husband, Bishop Williams, also comes to minister when I am unable to get back.

The schedule of an evangelist/pastor is quite demanding and can, at times, be overwhelming, but we who are committed to ministry welcome the opportunity to serve others. Often, after completing my ministerial duties for the day, it is late in the evening before I finally have an opportunity to sit down and eat my first meal. Not too long ago, after performing in concert Saturday night, I caught a flight home for Sunday morning service that started at 11:00 A.M. During that service, I led hymns, directed the choir, preached the sermon, ordained deacons, and afterward greeted all the members. Around 3:15 in the afternoon I gave the benediction, but my work for the day was just beginning.

One of the mothers of the church, Mae Littlejohn, was in the hospital and had been there for a few days. She is a very faithful member, so being out of worship service was alien to her. She missed the fellowship of the saints of God. With my church administrator, Carolyn Sanders, we drove to the hospital and took the elevator to the fifth floor and entered her room to visit and pray with her. We had only been there a few minutes when the door opened and about ten or twelve other members of our church came in. As we visited, I said to Mother Littlejohn, "Look, Mother, you couldn't come to church today, so we brought church to you. We're going to sing some songs for you." And we did. Our voices carried out into the hallway, and a few seconds later, a nurse opened the door slightly and looked in. For a moment, I thought she was going to tell us we had to be a little quieter, but she smiled instead. Going out, she left the door open. We kept on singing. A couple of minutes later, three or four other nurses stopped in front of the opened door, as did other patients who were walking the halls. Within moments, other patients came out of their rooms and stood in the hall to hear us sing. The presence of the Holy Spirit permeated Mother Littlejohn's room and filled the hospital corridors, touching the sick and encouraging and uplifting all who were present. It was almost 6:00 P.M. before we ended the hospital visitation and I took the time to eat.

At times I get a little beleaguered from the hectic schedule I keep. Being an evangelist, pastor, and gospel singer definitely takes a toll on one's body and vocal cords. But, in spite of those times when I experience complete exhaustion and occasional bouts of hoarseness, God has kept me strong and in good health. I praise Him that, in all my years of ministry, I've only experienced one episode of losing my voice, and then only because God was trying to tell me something.

In 1979, while feeling totally fatigued and physically depleted, I resolved that I would work smarter and not harder. I felt that if I cut back on preaching engagements and revival services and focused on incorporating sermonettes and altar calls during my concert performances, I could significantly decrease my travel itinerary and save much of my physical strength.

Immediately after making this decision to slow down, the Lord began to deal with me. There was uneasiness in my spirit that let me know something wasn't quite right. That feeling was confirmed the next weekend while I was performing in concert in New Orleans, Louisiana. We were headlining the concert and were scheduled to appear last on the program. While waiting for our curtain call, I sat in my dressing room fellowshiping with Leroy Johnson, whom I traveled with as a child, and some of the Caesar Singers. We were reminiscing about old times when someone came in and said, "Shirley, you're on next."

The temperature in the dressing room was about eighty degrees and a bit humid. The Caesar Singers and I immediately put on our stage attire and stood backstage waiting for our introduction. Once on stage I remember thinking to myself, It's a little chilly in here. It felt as though the thermostat was set around sixty degrees. Our opening song was "Miracle Worker." The first chorus went well, but when I opened my mouth to continue into the next chorus, nothing came out.

Realizing what was happening, two of my lead singers, Bernard Sterling and my sister Anne, took the song over. I kept trying, but to no avail. My voice was gone. I rationalized that this had happened because I had come from a warm, humid dressing room into a cold auditorium to sing and that the variation in temperatures was too much for my vocal cords. It was nothing to worry about, so I thought.

The next weekend we were in concert in Monticello, North Carolina, with about fifteen hundred people in attendance, and the power of God was being greatly manifested in that auditorium. We were nearing the end of the concert when I saw a lady in a wheelchair and felt a strong inclination to pray for her. As I prayed, God miraculously touched her body; she got out of the wheelchair and walked for the first time in her life. As she walked, I began to sing to her:

God's got it all in control.
He's got it all in control.
He put that reassurance, way down in my soul.
He's got it all in control.

After singing that stanza, I opened my mouth to sing the verse segment, but nothing came out. The same voice problem I experienced a week earlier in New Orleans had recurred. My rationale this time was that it must be my sinuses.

When the same scenario replayed itself for the third time at the conclusion of a concert in Houston, Texas, I decided it was time to seek medical attention. I had completely run out of reasons and rationales. I made an appointment with Frank Sinatra's throat specialist in New York City.

As the doctor examined me, he asked all kinds of questions.

"How often do you sing?"

"Quite often, usually over one hundred concerts annually."

"What kind of singer are you?"

"A gospel singer."

He examined my throat completely, then gave me his prognosis. "You have polyps on your vocal chords. I need to schedule you for surgery. We will first remove the polyps from the right side, let you recuperate from that, and then remove them from the left side."

I didn't like the sound of his prognosis or his remedy. To be quite honest, I really didn't think polyps were the real problem. Given the circumstances surrounding all that had happened with my voice, I was beginning to feel that the cause was more spiritual than natural. My mind kept going back to the fact that all my vocal problems began when I decided to cut back on preaching God's Word. Whenever we try to do things our way, and not according to God's plan, we inadvertently place ourselves outside His will and must suffer the consequences.

I knew what needed to be done, and surgery was not the answer. One Sunday morning, just before my pastor, Bishop Yelverton, preached, I asked him, "Will you pray for my throat?" I hadn't agreed to surgery but had begun taking the medication the specialist prescribed, and it was causing the texture of my voice to change. It was getting higher.

Bishop Yelverton called some of the praying mothers of the church to join him in prayer. Mother Briggs, Mother Walker, and Sister Sowell gathered around me; they anointed me with oil, and my pastor began to pray. I don't remember all that he said as he was talking to the Lord that morning, but I do know that while he was praying all I could hear in my spirit was *Preach or perish! Preach or perish!*

That was all the warning I needed. I knew I wasn't ready to die, so without question, I was definitely going to obey the voice of God. I immediately returned to my former method of ministry. I not only ministered in concerts, but I also reserved time to conduct regularly scheduled revival services. When I did, my throat problem instantly disappeared. If there was ever any doubt concerning my ministry, that whole experience confirmed unequivocally that the Lord had called me, a woman, to preach His Word and that nothing anyone could say or do would ever change that.

I accepted the pastorate of the Mount Calvary Word of Faith Church in August 1990. The Lord had actually placed this church and their pastor in my heart years prior to my accepting this commission. I had known and loved their pastor, Mother Elizabeth Lewis, for many years. She was also the National Church Mother of the Mount Calvary Holy Churches of America, Inc., and a dear mother in Zion who worked untiringly in God's vineyard, pastoring churches in both Richmond, Virginia, and Raleigh, North Carolina. From time to time I would preach for her congregations. I observed, firsthand, her labor of love and promised her that whenever she needed me, I would be there to assist in whatever way possible.

As she grew older and her health deteriorated to the point of incapacitation, it became impossible for her to commute weekly between Richmond, Virginia, and Raleigh, North Carolina, to minister to her congregations. In Mother Lewis's absence, the church in Raleigh was functioning without a pastor. Members such as Mother Mary Drakeford, Mother Dorothy Boykins, Deacon Frank Boykins, and others kept the church operative, holding daily prayer meetings and conducting weekly services. From time to time guest ministers were invited in to preach.

The state convocation of the Mount Calvary denomination convened in Durham, North Carolina, and while there the bishop's council met to determine the future of the Raleigh church. No one wanted the church to close; they wanted it to survive and again become a viable entity within the community.

When my husband returned from the meeting, I asked him, "What is the decision concerning the Raleigh church?"

He said, "We're going to ask Sister Deborah Yarborough to pastor the church."

I told him, "You can ask her if you want, but I can tell you now she's going to say no."

He was startled by my response. "What do you mean?"

"Well, the Lord told me that I would pastor that church. So she has to say no."

As he stated, Sister Yarborough was asked to become pastor of the Raleigh Mount Calvary Church. But guess what? She said no.

At that point they asked me to become the pastor, and I said yes!

Today, Pastor Deborah Yarborough-Obie serves as a copastor of the Durham Mount Calvary Church with her father, my former pastor, Bishop Frizelle Yelverton. The Lord's will in this area was realized in both our lives.

By the time I assumed the pastorate, the church had dwindled to seventeen members, including one deacon, one trustee, and four choir members.

Five members came to the church with me: my sister Anne Caesar Price, her husband, Eddie Price, Evangelist Carolyn Sanders, and my two nieces, Sharon Weaver and Cassietta Caesar. Immediately I held a "survival revival." I knew that revival was the key to the church's survival.

In my first sermon I told the congregation, "The Lord has given me a burden for this church. We're going to be a Word church. We're going to the college campuses. We're going into the streets. We're going after the dope pushers, the drug dealers. This little church is going to speak out! We're going into the enemy's camp and take back everything he has stolen from us. We're going to make a difference in this community."

I knew that's what the Lord was requiring of us—to speak out against evil, to speak out against sin, to speak out against the enemy. I grabbed the microphone that day and told the devil, "I command you in the name of Jesus to get your hat and coat and get out of here! We have no place for you in this church." And we didn't. The Lord would be with us and prosper us as we embarked upon a whole new ministry for Him.

I impressed upon the people that "although we might be a small church, we should consider ourselves numbered among the blessed, for God has richly blessed us. He has redeemed us, adopted us into His royal family, and made us citizens of heaven. We are heirs of the Father and joint heirs with the Son. We should never forget that."

I continued, "The road to heaven is not paved with biscuit wheels and gravy. You're going to cry sometimes; you're going to get sick sometimes. You're going to have trials and tribulations. I'm here to tell you to 'rejoice always, pray without ceasing, in everything give thanks; for this is the will of God in Christ Jesus for you.' You must take your eyes off yourself and put your eyes on the prize. And that prize is Jesus!"

We raised an offering every night that week. Not to compensate me. I told the people I wouldn't accept any salary for at least six months (and I still haven't to this day). Those offerings were taken to improve the conditions of the church. We replaced the worn-out carpeting and repainted the fading walls. The church had gone far too long without any maintenance work at all.

By the grace of God, the church survived. Ten new members joined that first week, and the church's growth has continued ever since. People began coming and getting saved. Some of the former members returned. Bible study became an intricate part of our weekly services. A new youth ministry was implemented, and we catered to the needs of our elderly.

I'm very much a hands-on pastor. I delegate, but I also participate. I assist in rehearsing the choirs, working with training the praise dancers, and teaching the youth. I'm there for counseling, advising, instructing, and doing everything necessary to care for the congregation the Lord has entrusted to me.

I realize that some people join the church with an ulterior motive, a hidden agenda. There have been some people who joined because of the personality instead of a real desire to worship the Lord in spirit and in truth. Those who do are soon disgruntled and become problem members. I don't worry about these kinds of people, because it has been my experience that the Lord will soon weed them out.

When I think about the church growth at Calvary, I know that some will say that the people are coming primarily to hear me sing. I don't have a problem with that because once they get in the building, along with hearing me sing they will also be hearing the word of God. Singing and preaching go together like ham and eggs. However, I honestly believe that the majority of the people come because they are hungry for the word of God.

People also come to our church because they enjoy the worship services. At Mount Calvary we believe in having old-fashioned church. We exemplify Nehemiah 8:10, which says in part, "The joy of the LORD is your strength." Therefore, singing, shouting, and dancing in the spirit are parts of our praise and worship to God. Not everyone understands our style of devotion, but David danced before the Lord, and Psalm 150 instructs us to, "Praise him with the sound of the trumpet: praise him with the psaltery and harp. Praise him with the timbrel and dance: praise him with stringed instruments and organs. Praise him upon loud cymbals: praise him upon the high sounding cymbals. Let everything that hath breath praise the LORD." (vv. 3-6 KJV)

I believe people also come because they see our church demonstrating a genuine concern for the community, especially for the elderly. A pastor has the responsibility of trying to meet the needs of people everywhere—the needs of the people in the pews and those in the streets, the saint and the sinner, the homeless and the shut-in.

God has a financial plan for the church—tithes and offerings. I'm not against churches that try to subsidize themselves by selling dinners, sponsoring car washes, and conducting other fund-raisers; they are also part of our church's fund-raising activities. But God's financial plan for the church involves tithes and offerings, so I teach our congregation to be a tithing church. God has promised in Malachi 3:10 that if you will bring your tithe (10 percent of your increase), and your offering, He will "open for you the windows of heaven / And pour out for you such blessing / That there will not be room enough to receive it."

Many believe this is only an Old Testament doctrine. However, I often counter that belief with something Pastor Richard D. Hinton of the Monument of Faith Church in Chicago says, "I'd rather get to heaven and find out that I didn't have to pay my tithes than to get to heaven and find out that I should have paid them and didn't."

Mount Calvary's policy for helping people is not predicated upon denomination or church affiliation. We don't ask about someone's religion or religious affiliation before we help them. We tell them about Jesus, but we don't turn anyone away simply because they don't share our particular religious beliefs. Attending to their natural needs gives us the avenue to minister to their spiritual needs.

It is very difficult to tell a person that Jesus is the bread of life when they are starving. However, once you feed them natural food, then you can share the spiritual bread of life with them.

By the same token, it is not enough just to feed a person one meal. Our objective is to enhance a person's life by equipping them to provide for themselves. If a person wants to learn to read, we tutor him. If he needs a job, we assist in job placement. We believe that if you give someone a fish, he eats for one day, but if you teach him how to fish, he eats every day. Our goal is not to give a handout, but to give a hand. You should never look down on a man unless you are picking him up.

I have a tremendous burden for the youth of our nation. Gang violence, drugs, crime, and teenage pregnancy are running rampant. We must do something about this epidemic.

At the 1996 Grammy Awards, during my performance, my manager, Carolyn Sanders, went to take my assigned seat in the audience next to my husband. When she got there the rappers Tupac Shakur and Snoop Doggie Dogg and their bodyguard were sitting in the section. One of them was in my seat. She approached them and said, "I'm sorry, but one of you is sitting in my seat."

The bodyguard became quite belligerent. "This isn't your seat," he protested.

Bishop Williams was seated next to him. "Yes, it is," he said. "This is my wife's manager, and you're in my wife's seat."

The bodyguard kept protesting, "We aren't moving."

"We'll just have to get an usher," Bishop Williams replied.

Then Tupac gently replied, "Ma'am, take my seat." He told his bodyguard, "Come on, leave it alone. These are their seats. Let's go." Carolyn said that unlike the bodyguard, Tupac was very courteous and a perfect gentleman. It was obvious he was not the villain that the media had portrayed him to be. Tragically, just a few weeks later, someone shot and killed Tupac. His was a senseless death that should not have occurred.

We must reach our youth. Many of them are on a downward spiral; they terrorize our neighborhoods, making them unsafe. Our elderly are afraid to be out after dark. Some youth are strung out on drugs and alcohol. Eleven-year-old girls, still babies themselves, are having babies. Bars are on our windows, and padlocks are on our doors. Guns are on the streets, and our youth are being shot down like animals. My heart is heavy, and my spirit is grieved.

For two consecutive Sundays, I stood in my pulpit, weeping over what I saw in our communities across the nation. I prayed and prayed, "Lord, what can I do, how can I make a difference?"

In response, the Lord immediately dropped the answer in my spirit. I needed to begin ministering to our youth, talking explicitly to them, and in return I needed to let them talk to me while I listened to their hurts, their concerns, and their fears. I began doing this in my church, in my concerts, and in my recordings.

First, I initiated Children's Time at Mount Calvary. This is where we take time out of every Sunday morning worship service to talk directly to our young people. We tell them that they do not have to succumb to peer pressure, that they can be somebody, and that they can succeed in life. We stress the fact that *Jesus* plus *education* equals *success*.

In concerts I make a special point to tell the young people, "If you want to work for McDonald's all your life, drop out of school. If you want to own a McDonald's franchise, stay in school. Don't be the class clown; be the class valedictorian." I tell them, "When I was growing up, I had to ride in the back of the bus, but today I have my own bus."

I remind them, "Just because you came from the ghetto doesn't mean you have to stay in the ghetto. You may live in the ghetto, but you don't have to let the ghetto live in you.

You can be anybody you want. If you want to be a bum, that's what you'll be, but if you want to be the president of a major corporation, you can achieve that also. You don't have to end up pregnant, on drugs, or incarcerated. With God's help you can be anything you want to be."

We must find a way to take our youth back from the clutches of drugs, alcohol, and violence. The church must get involved in this battle. Wouldn't it be wonderful if all of our churches had an outreach ministry that would take the gospel to the streets, carrying the message to the youth who won't come to the church?

When I recall my own childhood, I see a young girl who came from a long line of poor folk. I had no idea what my destiny would be. When I graduated from high school, some people didn't think I would go very far.

Every year at graduation, the school gave each of the seniors a little present, which was supposed to depict their special talent. The teachers gave me a tuning fork because I loved music so much. They knew that all I ever wanted to be was a gospel singer. The teachers knew it; everybody knew it. By the grace of God I turned that tuning fork into nine Grammy Awards and a ministry of winning souls to Jesus Christ. As the apostle Paul says, "To live is Christ, and to die is gain."

While I travel on this earth, "If I can help somebody as I pass this way; if I can show someone they're going astray; if I can spread this ministry from day to day, then my living will not be in vain."

CHAPTER THIRTEEN

We're Going to Have Church

THE MELODY

I'm seeking all my treasures up in glory;
for heaven is the place I want to be.
Jesus will be waiting up in glory.
Come on and go with me over there,
over there, over there,
Come and go with me over there.
We'll be singing, we'll be shouting,
we're going to tell the world all about it.
Come on and go with me over there.
—"Come Go with Me"

AND THE WORD

The hour is coming, and now is,
when the true worshipers will worship the Father
in spirit and truth;
for the Father is seeking such to worship Him.
God is Spirit, and those who worship Him must worship
in spirit and truth.
—John 4:23–24

193

In January 1981 the Caesar Singers and I traveled to New York City to participate in a weekend production called "Get on Board! A Holiday Gospel Celebration," which was presented by the Brooklyn Academy of Music. Each night a different form of music was presented, from jazz to classical to gospel.

As the featured gospel artists, we performed on Saturday night. When I walked onto the stage, I asked the audience, "How many of you came to have church tonight?"

In an instant the audience responded with a loud shout.

I love it when the audience is enthusiastic and energetic, for it makes my job of ministering to them easy and enjoyable. Whether in concert performance or revival services, I always seek to involve the audience or the congregation, because the more they participate, the more their faith is elevated, and the easier it is for them to receive what they are seeking from the Lord. An open and receptive audience affords the Holy Spirit the opportunity to move freely among the people. In many of our concerts, where the Holy Spirit is uninhibited, I've seen those who couldn't walk get out of wheelchairs, those who were deaf receive their hearing, and those with impaired vision receive their sight. The Spirit of God moves among those who exemplify faith, and to stimulate the faith of the congregation I often relate my personal testimony of how the Lord healed me of glaucoma and kidney stones. I then remind them that "if God can do it for me, He can do it for anyone."

I realize that people have needs and expectations that only God can provide, so in every service it is my endeavor to lead them into the very presence of the Lord. I'm often asked how do I maintain such a high level of energy during concerts. My response is, I give all that I humanly can and then I rely upon the Holy Spirit to strengthen and anoint me for service. Sometimes, even I am amazed at how I keep going.

One Sunday afternoon after completing a concert in Charlotte, North Carolina, we rushed to another concert scheduled in Shelby, North Carolina. There was no time to stop and eat because we had to be there by 7:30 that evening. Arriving a little behind schedule, we had a quick sound check and immediately prepared to go on stage. As always, we held corporate prayer.

Right in the middle of the concert, as we were singing "Sweeping Through the City," I noticed something was happening among my three background singers. Our soprano, Suella Colbert, was standing between Bernard Sterling and my sister Anne, swaying back and forth as though her equilibrium was unbalanced. I continued to sing, but when I looked back again, Suella had completely slumped over on Anne. She continued to slump farther and farther to the side until Anne and Bernard were literally holding her up. I thought she was overcome by the power of God.

By this time, I noticed that everyone in the audience had stopped listening to us and was watching her.

I said to the audience, "She's all right. Don't worry about her; that's just the Holy Ghost."

While still singing and praising the Lord, Anne discreetly moved toward me. I could see she wanted to say something. I leaned my head toward her.

She said, "That's not the Holy Ghost, that's the Hungry Ghost!"

I nearly fell over laughing. I knew she was right. We had not eaten all day. We were hungry. In fact, we were famished and tired.

Perseverance and stamina were traits that I noticed in the gospel singers who frequently came to our church during my childhood days. I would eagerly watch them as they inspired the congregation. It was amazing to observe how they bridged the gap between their music and their message. Sitting on that church pew watching them, I knew I wanted to do the same, and I have tried to emulate that in my ministry. I work to develop a rhythm between singing and preaching because preaching provides the bridge to the song. In essence, in my concerts the audience truly receives the melody and the word. Only the anointing of the Lord makes this happen. If God doesn't anoint what I'm doing, then no effort I put forth can make any difference.

When I go into an area for a concert, I generally inquire as to which of my recordings the gospel announcers are airing in order to get an idea of which songs the audience may want to hear. In concert, however, I always stay sensitive to the leading of the Holy Spirit so that I may be responsive to the needs of the people. Sometimes by the prompting of the Holy Spirit I will say to the audience, "I hear a song ringing in my spirit," or "I want to tell you a story."

Many of the stories I relate come out of my life experiences with the Lord and my family. Others are stories based on current issues that people are facing. Jesus always spoke in parables, and I pattern myself after Him. Any time I relate a story about other incidents or myself, it opens the door for me to emphasize a spiritual reality.

When I speak to children about how, as a child, I stole Popsicles, threw rocks at streetlights, and talked back to my mother, they can relate to these experiences and realize that although we are disobedient and rebellious, Jesus still loves us and will forgive us.

When I share with men and women the grief I experienced upon my mother's death, they empathize with me because most have lost loved ones also. Consequently, when

I tell them that "earth has no sorrow that heaven cannot heal" and that the Lord will see them through their grief, they realize that I know firsthand that God is able to take the hurt out of the hurt and the pain out of the pain.

Many of the parables I relate are the basis for several of the songs I record. For example, a woman who wants to backslide, because she feels that God has forsaken her, forms the story line for the song "Don't Give Up." The lady in the neighborhood who degrades a so-called bad girl who lives down the street from her is the theme for the song "Be Careful of the Stones You Throw." And the story of Shouting John who doesn't have the freedom to praise the Lord in the dead church to which he belongs is the framework for the song "Hold My Mule."

In 1984 I had the privilege of traveling to the Middle East with a group of singers that included Andrae Crouch, Barry White, and James Cleveland. This was my first trip to the Holy Land, and quite naturally I was very excited about touring the ancient city of Jerusalem where Jesus had walked and performed many miracles during His ministry on earth. I took a taxi to many of the historical sites, including the Wailing Wall (which is called the Western Wall), the Garden of Gethsemane, and the *empty* tomb of Jesus.

During the tour the cab driver and I began to talk. He told me all about Jerusalem, its traditions and customs. I told him we were there to perform a gospel concert. When he found out I was a Christian, he warned me, "If I were you, I wouldn't talk about Jesus in Jerusalem, because He was a troublemaker. Whatever you do, remember, don't talk about Jesus in Jerusalem." Coming from him, I felt that was an ironic statement to make. For just a moment earlier he was telling me of the miracle that was wrought during the crucifixion of Jesus. He had explained that when Jesus was carrying the cross to Calvary, as He struggled, the soldiers called Simon of Cyrene, an egg bearer, to carry the cross for Him. Simon sat his egg basket down and picked up the cross. When he returned from Jesus' crucifixion, each egg had turned a different color. The cab driver went on to explain that this was the origination of Easter eggs.

So when he told me to not mention Jesus' name, I couldn't believe what I was hearing. I thought to myself, Here in the Holy Land! Here where Jesus had lived, died, and rose again! How could I not talk about Him?

That night we performed a concert in Jerusalem at an outdoor stadium called Sultan's Pool. People were everywhere, sitting on the hillsides and standing on the plains. As I started to sing, I kept thinking about the cab driver's warning.

Our first song was "No Charge." And the Israelis thoroughly enjoyed that selection. When I began singing "Miracle Worker," I realized that in order to sing this song I would have to call the name of Jesus, loud and long.

When I came to the place in the song where I call upon the name of Jesus, instead of saying *Jesus*, I initially tried to substitute by shouting out the words *power* and *holy*, over and over again. But the Holy Spirit within me said, *If you're ashamed to own Me before these people in Israel, then I'll be ashamed to own you before my Father in heaven.*

Right then I threw my head back and began to shout as loud as I could, "Jesus, Jesus, Jesus!"

I didn't stop calling His name. In fact, as I called the name of Jesus, I held the microphone out toward the audience, and they shouted His name with me. The words of the cab driver were no longer ringing in my ear, instead all I could hear was, "There is power in the name of Jesus."

I'll never forget the thrill of hearing those thousands of

Jews call the name of Jesus. Who would have thought that Jews in Jerusalem would actually proclaim the name of Jesus! I love it when the Holy Spirit does the unexpected. There was absolutely no way of my knowing when I stepped on stage that such a phenomenal occurrence would take place. I don't ever want to get so rehearsed or so routine in my performance that I can't respond to the way the Holy Spirit is leading the service. It's very seldom that I sing a song the same way every time. Even if it's only a slight variation, the Holy Spirit will give me something distinctly different, which will meet the needs of those in the audience. As a result, my concerts are just as impromptu and innovative to me as they are for my audiences. Although there are certain songs and stories that I customarily perform in concert, the sequences, the dynamics, and the general feeling of a song are always different.

The sole purpose of ministry, whether singing or preaching, is to lead men and women to Jesus Christ, to bring them into a knowledge of His saving grace. With that purpose in mind, I never close a concert without an altar call. After I have spoken directly from my heart to the audience, and ministered to them through a parable, personal experience, or song, I would be remiss in my calling as a minister of the gospel, if I did not give them the opportunity to respond. Often, the Holy Spirit will make His own altar call. I can always sense when that is about to occur. Usually it is after a song has so touched and convicted the hearts of the people that they are automatically drawn into an atmosphere of praise and worship unto God. And when people begin to worship the Lord in spirit and in truth, deliverance is imminent and souls will be saved, bodies will be healed, drug addicts and alcoholics will be delivered, and problems will be solved. It is exhilarating to witness this pinnacle of praise and worship because when this occurs, believe you me, it is no longer necessary to elicit a response from the audience, for they are spontaneously on their feet, glorifying and magnifying the Lord.

One such incident occurred while we were performing at the Apollo Theater in New York City along with Dorothy Norwood and the Mighty Clouds of Joy. That particular night I witnessed a phenomenal move of God that was utterly spectacular. I can't remember the song we were singing, but I do know that the presence and the anointing of the Holy Spirit came so forcefully in the auditorium that it was overwhelming. People all over the auditorium simultaneously began to shout accolades of praise unto God. Many were crying tears of joy. Others came running to the front of the stage wanting to dedicate their lives to Christ, while still more came rushing toward us onstage, wanting to shake our hands. Out of all the times I had performed at the Apollo, I had never seen the Lord bless the people so abundantly, not even when I was with the Caravans. I must admit that with so many people in one place, all of them so excited, and with hundreds of them coming toward us on the stage, I became a bit apprehensive. The theater personnel, unfamiliar with the outpouring of the Holy Spirit, misinterpreted what was taking place. Thinking that a riot was about to erupt, they turned off the theater lights to keep the people from storming onto the stage. Even in the dark you could hear shouts of praise and adoration reverberating throughout the building.

The move of God is not restricted by place, circumstances, or environment. This fact was again profoundly demonstrated during the time I performed in the Broadway musical, *Mama, I Want to Sing*. What I thought would be just a rote stage performance turned out to be a great manifestation of the power of God.

Vi Higginsen initially asked me to appear in her production in 1993, but I was unable to accept because of a conflict of scheduling. However, she kept asking, and finally dates were selected that would allow me to accept her offer. The script portrayed the story of a young girl, Doris Winter, who grew up in a very religious family. Her father was a preacher who died while preaching in the pulpit when Doris was just a child. She was blessed with a beautiful voice, and her mother wanted her to use it exclusively in the service of the Lord. Doris, on the other hand, wanted to achieve fame and fortune through singing secular music.

The character I portrayed was that of Sister Carrie, an outspoken, openhearted, and forthright lady who dearly loved her god-daughter, Doris. Because our characters were so similar in nature, I didn't think I would have a problem projecting Sister Carrie on stage. However, the church scenes were of great concern to me, because I knew I could never "play" church. There was no way I could ever pretend to be under the influence of the Holy Spirit when I wasn't.

Those early rehearsals initially caused me a great deal of anxiety. The songs weren't an issue because I simply sang them with the same fervency and intensity I put into all my songs, but remembering my lines posed a problem. A stage production is predicated upon a set script. There is very little room for spontaneity, and I am a very spontaneous person. I invariably say what fits the circumstances and the scene. I have to admit there were times when I meant to say one line but something else automatically came out. I thought the producers would be upset, but they actually encouraged me. They said, "Pastor Caesar, just be yourself." As the old folks would say, "They just should not have told me that." From that point on, I didn't worry. I just let the Lord have His way. And night after night, I witnessed the presence of the Lord moving throughout that auditorium blessing those in attendance. Obviously Vi Higginsen and the producers were pleased with the outcome, because they invited me back for three other appearances on Broadway in subsequent productions of the *Mama, I Want to Sing* trilogy: *Mama 2, Born to Sing,* and *This Is My Song.* During my tenure with these productions, I had the privilege of performing and interacting with several other gifted singers and actresses including Stephanie Mills, Desiree Coleman-Jackson, Regina Belle, Doris Troy, and Asa Dosreis.

I had the freedom to do in those productions the same as I would do in any revival or concert appearance. At the end of each performance I had the opportunity to speak directly to the audience, letting them know that even though this was a play, there was a profound spiritual lesson to be learned. I appealed to them either to accept, return, or rededicate their lives to Christ. Whenever and wherever God opens a door and gives you a platform to witness for Him, always avail yourself of the opportunity. Because when it is all said and done, it is only what we do for Christ that will last.

CHAPTER FOURTEEN

Witness for the Lord

THE MELODY

Heaven, heaven, I'm going there.
Oh, heaven, heaven, I'm going there.
When the Lord shall crack the sky,
I'm going to my home on high.
Now the Lord doesn't want any man to perish.
He's so kind.
Take advantage of your time.
Oh, it won't be long, we'll be going home.
Over in heaven.
To a city called heaven, I'm going there.
I'll never cry no more, I'm going there.
I'll never die no more, I'm going there.
Joy over there.
Peace over there.
Love over there.
To a city called heaven, I'm going there.
—"Heaven"

‖‖‖‖‖‖‖‖‖‖‖ AND THE WORD ‖‖‖‖‖‖‖‖‖‖‖‖‖‖

Now I saw a new heaven and a new earth,
for the first heaven and the first earth had passed away.
Also there was no more sea. Then I, John, saw the holy city,
New Jerusalem, coming down out of heaven from God,
prepared as a bride adorned for her husband.
And I heard a loud voice from heaven saying,
"Behold, the tabernacle of God is with men,
and He will dwell with them, and they shall be His people.
God Himself will be with them and be their God.
And God will wipe away every tear from their eyes;
there shall be no more death, nor sorrow, nor crying.
There shall be no more pain,
for the former things have passed away."
—Revelation 21:1–4

———— OVER six thousand people, including many of the major celebrities from home and abroad had gathered in the beautiful Los Angeles Shrine Auditorium for the greatest musical event of the year, the Grammy Awards, the Oscars of the music world. Everyone was eloquently dressed, the women in evening attire created by high-fashion designers, and the men in both traditional and contemporary tuxedos. There were young people who had decided to make a fashion statement by dressing in blue jeans, tuxedo tails, and tennis shoes, but even they appeared suave and debonair. It was the thirty-eighth annual Grammy Awards, presented by the National Academy of Recording Arts and Sciences (NARAS), and this year over thirty million people would be watching the ceremony on national television.

Standing offstage, my heart pounding, I waited for my time to perform. With great anticipation, I watched and listened as Whitney Houston, dressed in a gorgeous chocolate, ankle-length gown, walked onto the stage. Her elegant presence and magnificent voice added an undeniable distinction to the evening. To my delight, the talent committee for the Grammy Awards had asked Whitney to perform a salute to gospel music, and she, in turn, had requested CeCe Winans and myself to join her in making that happen. I was ecstatic. This was a God-given opportunity to share Jesus with the world!

Her melodious voice extending over the audience, Whitney began the introduction to the set of songs that would spotlight gospel music. She said, "Gospel music is the music I love the best. It gave me my roots. Gospel is a true gift from God, and we sing it to give glory to Him. It lives on not just in the churches but also because it was a forerunner to rhythm and blues, jazz, rock, and other popular music. Gospel is sung by some of music's best and most beloved performers."

Hearing her speak, I found myself nodding in agreement. Gospel is the root of African-American musicians. It was the church that gave us our first platform to practice and perfect our gifts. In our lives and in the lives of millions of others who listen to and appreciate this art form, gospel music lives.

It didn't take long for Whitney and CeCe to mesmerize the audience. CeCe first warmed their hearts by singing in her wonderful style "I Surrender All." Her rich voice immediately captured attention.

Listening to her, I couldn't believe the opportunity afforded us to offer such a powerful witness for the Lord on national television. Far too often, programs try to do just the opposite. They attempt to present Jesus in a negative light, discredit the church, and make mockery of the people of faith.

But not tonight. Tonight before millions, we would have the privilege to present Jesus in a positive manner.

As CeCe finished her song, Whitney moved onstage to join her. Seamlessly, showcasing the incredible talents God had given her, Whitney moved into a duet with CeCe, a powerful arrangement of "Count on Me." The audience sat in awe as these two talented young women sang.

Standing backstage, I also listened, enjoying every word. I could hardly wait to join them.

As CeCe and Whitney neared the end of their duet, I took a deep breath, smoothed my skirt, made sure my hair was in place, squared the shoulders of my suit jacket, and said a prayer. In just a couple of moments, I would have the opportunity along with Whitney and CeCe to be a witness for the Lord before millions of people watching the telecast.

I prayed and asked the Lord to anoint me in demonstrating to the world what a joy it is to know Him, not only in the fellowship of His suffering, but also in the power of His resurrection. In those moments, standing backstage, the events of this incredible day flashed through my mind. One incident stood out above all others. Earlier that evening I had received my eighth Grammy Award.

To keep the Grammy Award's production within the allocated broadcast time, only a select number of music categories are earmarked for award presentation during the live telecast. All other categories are awarded during a pre-telecast ceremony, and the winners are shown on still frame throughout the live telecast. As it turned out, the presentation of the category in which I was nominated, Best Traditional Soul Gospel Album, took place during the pre-telecast segment.

The fact that I didn't receive my eighth Grammy on live television really didn't matter. Just winning again, and knowing that I would perform later, was reward enough.

Sitting in the audience with my husband, Bishop Harold Williams, my manager, Carolyn Sanders, and songwriter Michael Mathis awaiting the announcement of the winner, I felt tense and apprehensive. This was my fifteenth nomination, and I had seven prior wins, but regardless of how many times I had previously won, when it came to this moment, my heart always began racing wildly.

Surviving the nominating procedure is complimentary enough, but actually winning gives an ultimate sense of satisfaction and achievement. The nominating process begins when individual record companies and other industry representatives submit to the Academy all eligible releases that meet the nominating guidelines. Next, over one hundred NARAS board representatives screen the eligible releases for proper category placement (rock, country, jazz, rap, classical, gospel).

First-round ballots are then sent to all voting members of the Academy to vote in ten of the twenty-one possible categories. This vote determines the list of five finalists from each category. A second ballot of category finalists is sent to Academy members for voting. This second voting determines the winners. Independent accounting firms tabulate each set of ballots.

For a musician, there is no greater award than the Grammy. To be voted by your peers and industry representatives as the most outstanding in your musical field is the ultimate honor you can receive for all your efforts, including writing and choosing the right songs, collaborating with producers, and working long, tedious hours in recording and mixing the final project.

I am always cognizant of the fact that whenever I am nominated for such a prestigious award, it is only by the grace of God, because certainly there were other recordings just as deserving as mine. But here I was again, by the unmerited favor of God, sitting in the midst of thousands of people waiting for the announcement of the Grammy Award for the Best Traditional Soul Gospel Album of the year. I was optimistic that my recording, *Shirley Caesar Live . . . He Will Come*, had a fair chance of winning, but at the same time I didn't want to build my hopes up for a possible letdown.

As the presenters moved down the categories of awards, I felt my anxiety mounting more and more. Again, I scanned the list of the other nominees in my category. They were all wonderful musicians and great performers. Could I possibly win again? I reached over and squeezed my husband's hand.

Finally, I heard my category announced. My heart was pounding as the presenter called out the names of the nominees. I held my breath as he opened the envelope and pulled out the winner's name. For a moment it seemed like time stood still. Then I heard the words, "And the winner is, *Shirley Caesar Live . . . He Will Come!*"

With a prayer of thanksgiving and a shout of joy, I hugged my husband and ran onto the stage. As I received that award, I held it close to my heart. "I thank God for blessing me to receive such a prestigious award," I said. "For without Him I can do nothing. To God be the glory." I then expressed gratitude to those who had helped make this moment a reality: the staff members at Word Records; my manager, Carolyn Sanders; my songwriter, Michael Mathis; and my executive producer and coproducer, Chuck Myricks and Bubba Smith. I wanted them to know how much their diligence, loyalty, and support meant to me. I never could have done it without them.

All around me, cameras flashed and people applauded. Smiling, I couldn't help thinking just how far the Lord had brought me. As I exited the stage, I again silently told the Lord how much I loved Him!

Now as I stood backstage reminiscing the events that had taken place earlier, I somehow knew that the remainder of the night would be even more memorable.

The sound of Whitney Houston introducing me broke my chain of thoughts.

"Are you ready?" Whitney shouted to the audience.

"Yes!" they shouted back.

She said again, "Are you ready?"

They yelled, "Yes!"

She said, "You'd better get ready, get ready for the First Lady of Gospel Music, the great Shirley Caesar!"

The time had come, my cue had been given. With a joyful smile, I ran onto the stage. Whitney and CeCe and Hezekiah Walker and the Love Fellowship Gospel Choir backed me up. We sang one of my favorite songs, "Heaven." The words speak of the joy of going to heaven when the Lord returns in the Rapture:

> *Heaven, heaven, I'm going there.*
> *Heaven, heaven, I'm going there.*
> *When the Lord shall crack the sky,*
> *I'm going to my home on high.*
> *To a city called heaven.*
> *I'm going there.*

Everyone immediately stood. Some were shouting, others were praising the Lord, most were singing, and some just swayed to the rhythm of the music. It was heaven on earth in that auditorium. As I poured my heart into the song, I felt the Holy Spirit take control. I knew that He was achieving His purpose in the hearts and minds of those in attendance and those watching on national television. Even now, as I meet people they tell me how they felt the power of God coming through their television set as we sang "Heaven" at the Grammy Awards. Yes, I was thankful for the eighth Grammy Award I had won that evening, but I was eternally grateful for the opportunity to share Jesus with the world!

My greatest joy in life is being a minister of the gospel. People often ask me how long I plan to keep traveling, preaching, and singing for the Lord. I always respond by telling them, "I will be singing and preaching as long as the Lord gives me the health and strength to do so. And if it is His will, I don't plan on retiring any time soon."

I am flattered by those who say that I seem to get younger and younger as the years go by. I thank them for their generosity. And to those who overtly ask my age, I playfully answer, "I'm too young for Medicare and too old for you to care." But, all teasing aside, it is my earnest prayer that God will bless me with longevity so that I may accomplish more for His kingdom. I know that heaven is a beautiful place, and I long to go there. But I also know that souls are dying without Jesus in their lives, and I must do all I can to win as many souls to Christ as possible. Like the apostle Paul, I believe "To live is Christ, and to die is gain."

There are still many objectives in life that I am striving to achieve. To some they may sound far-fetched and unrealistic, but "I can do all things through Christ who strengthens me." I have often thought about adopting children. Coming from a large family, I experienced firsthand the life and joy that children bring to a home. Certainly, somewhere there is a child who would love to have me as a mother. (Smile.)

Returning to graduate school to pursue my master's degree in divinity is another goal of mine. It is never too late to expand and improve your knowledge, and I desire a thorough and comprehensive understanding of God's Word. Also, God has given me a vision for our church. He has already blessed us with ten acres of land, and very shortly we will begin building a new church edifice that will seat at least twelve hundred people. Over the last seven years our church membership has literally outgrown our facilities, creating a dire need for expansion. But the edifice is just the first phase of the vision. We also have plans to erect a senior citizens' complex. When I think of all the elderly who live alone without any family or friends to love and care for them, my heart is saddened. The church has a responsibility to contribute actively to the protection and shelter of the elderly, and I'm determined that our church shall do its part.

In addition to a senior citizens' complex, I foresee establishing a Bible training institute to provide training for young men and women desiring to enter the ministry.

Last but not least, I would love to implement a Christian academy for kindergarten through twelfth grade. It would emphasize academics and religious education, thereby preparing our students for college and practical living while simultaneously teaching them God's Word. This school would provide a controlled environment where students would be free from the outside forces of drug pushers, gang violence, and peer pressure.

The vision and plans I have for the future are extensive, but they are attainable. God has promised that whatsoever we desire when we pray, believe and He shall bring it to pass. I have faith that God will bring every component of this vision into fruition. There may be some delays, but circumstances or delays do not shake faith. And when every aspect of this vision shall have been realized, God will give new inspiration, new ideas, and new visions. Without a vision, the people will perish.

Occasionally, I've been asked to voice my opinion about the current state of gospel music and whether or not new singers intimidate me. Without hesitation, I respond, "Definitely not." We are all colaborers in the gospel. We are all engaged in a spiritual warfare, to combat Satan with every tool we have available. We must fight him until we can't fight anymore. Our songs are a powerful weapon against Satan. I thank God for all the new gospel singers, new recruits in the army of the Lord, coming on the scene to join forces in this war. The enemy has something on his hands. And where I leave off, others will rise to take my place.

As for now, my ministry on earth is not finished. And as long as there is breath in my body, I will continue to be a person of melody, singing the praises of the Lord, and a person of the Word, proclaiming the gospel of Jesus Christ. I will continue to do God's will and always remain true to my gospel roots. As a soldier of the Cross, I will not compromise the gospel.

The lyrics to the song "Heaven" describe my perspective on life. Whatever I accomplish materially here on earth is temporary. Heaven for me is not awards; it isn't money or fame. Heaven is not winning eight, ten, or twenty Grammy Awards. Heaven is love, joy, peace, and happiness in Christ Jesus!

Only what we do for Christ will last. When the summation of our deeds on earth has been evaluated at the judgment seat of Christ, none of it will matter, if our names aren't written in the Lamb's Book of Life. More than anything else, I want to hear my Savior say, "Well done, good and faithful servant; you were faithful over a few things, I will make you ruler over many things. Enter into the joy of your Lord."

APPENDIX

DISCOGRAPHY

1967 *Shirley Caesar*
I'll Go
Hob Records

1968 *Shirley Caesar*
Jordan River
Hob Records

1969 *Shirley Caesar*
Inspirations
Hob Records

1970 *Shirley Caesar*
Get Up, My Brother
Hob Records

1970 *Shirley Caesar*
Millennial Reign
Hob Records

1971 *Shirley Caesar*
My Testimony
Hob Records

1973 Shirley Caesar
Three Old Men
Hob Records

1974 Shirley Caesar and James Cleveland
King and Queen of Gospel Vol. 1 & Vol. 2
Hob Records

1975 Shirley Caesar
Go Take a Bath
Hob Records

1975 Shirley Caesar
Be Careful of the Stones You Throw
Hob Records

1977 Shirley Caesar
Shirley Caesar's Greatest Hits
Vesta Records

1977 Shirley Caesar and James Cleveland
Our Greatest Hits
Vesta Records

1977 Shirley Caesar
First Lady
Roadshow Records

1978 Shirley Caesar
From the Heart
Roadshow Records

1978 Shirley Caesar
Shirley Caesar Sings Her Gospel Favorites
Spire Records

1980 Shirley Caesar
Rejoice
Word Records

1981 Shirley Caesar
Go
Word Records

1982 Shirley Caesar
Jesus, I Love Calling Your Name
Word Records

1984 Shirley Caesar
Sailin'
Word Records

1985 Shirley Caesar
Celebration
Word Records

1986 Shirley Caesar
Christmasing
Word Records

1987 Shirley Caesar
Her Very Best
Word Records

1988 Shirley Caesar
Live . . . in Chicago
Word Records

1989 Shirley Caesar
I Remember Mama
Word Records

1991 Shirley Caesar
He's Working It Out for You
Word Records

1993 Shirley Caesar
Stand Still
Word/Epic Records

1995 Shirley Caesar
Shirley Caesar Live . . . He Will Come
1996 Shirley Caesar Outreach Convention Choir
Just a Word
Word/Epic Records

1997 Shirley Caesar
A Miracle in Harlem
Word/Epic Records

VIDEO DISCOGRAPHY

1988 Live in Memphis . . . Hold My Mule
Word Records

1989 I Remember Mama
Word Records

1996 Shirley Caesar Live . . . He Will Come
Word/Epic Records